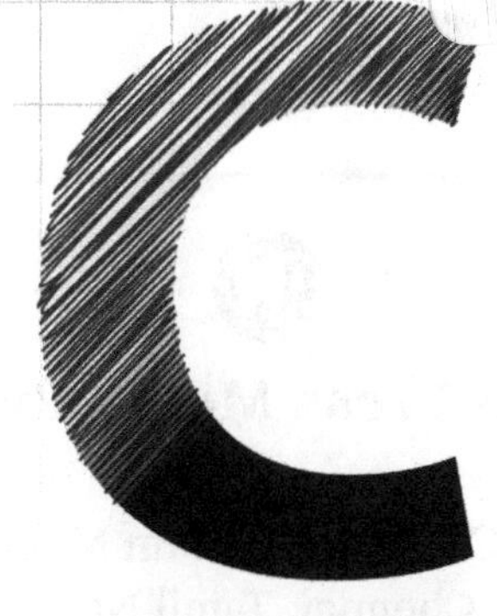

C THE BASICS

A STEP-BY-STEP TO LEARN AND PRACTICE C-PROGRAMMING

SEELAM SAI SATYANARAYANA REDDY, MUKKALA ANANDA RANJITH KUMAR

INDIA • SINGAPORE • MALAYSIA

Notion Press Media Pvt Ltd

No. 50, Chettiyar Agaram Main Road,
Vanagaram, Chennai, Tamil Nadu – 600 095

First Published by Notion Press 2021

ISBN 978-1-63904-529-7

C THE BASICS

Dr. Seelam Sai Satyanarayana Reddy,
Professor & Principal, Sreyas Institute of Engineering & Technology, Hyd, T. S.

Mukkala Ananda Ranjith Kumar,
Assoc. Professor, Sreyas Institute of Engineering & Technology, Hyd, T. S.

Contents

CHAPTER 1	**Introduction to Computers**	**9**
1.1	Basics	9
	1.1.1 Hardware	11
	1.1.2 Software	16
1.2	Computing Environments	23
1.3	Computer Languages	25
1.4	Introduction to Problem Solving	29
	1.4.1 Algorithm Development	29
	1.4.2 Flowchart	34
1.5	Program Development Life Cycle (or) Software Development Life Cycle (SDLC)	37
CHAPTER 2	**Introduction to C Programming**	**41**
2.1	History	41
2.2	C Tokens	44
2.3	Key Words	47
2.4	Data Types in C	49
2.5	Different Statements	51
2.6	Structure of a C program	53
2.7	Creating and Running a C Program	55
CHAPTER 3	**Operators in C**	**57**
3.1	Introduction	57
3.2	Operators Precedence in C	67

3.3	Expressions and it's Evaluation	68
3.4	Input Output Functions in C	72
	3.4.1 Formatted Input/Output Functions	72
	3.4.2 Unformatted I/O Function	79
3.5	Type Conversion in C	83
CHAPTER 4	**Statements**	**85**
4.1	Introduction	85
4.2	Types of Statements	85
4.3	Conditional Statements	87
4.4	Looping Statements	99
	4.4.1 While Loop	101
	4.4.2 Do While Loop	105
	4.4.3 For Loop	106
	4.4.4 Nested Loops	112
4.5	Jump Statements	116
CHAPTER 5	**Arrays**	**119**
5.1	Introduction	119
5.2	One Dimensional Arrays	119
5.3	Applications of an Array	125
5.4	Two Dimensional Arrays (2D arrays)	131
5.5	Multi Dimensional Arrays	141
CHAPTER 6	**Strings**	**145**
6.1	Introduction	145
6.2	String Handling Functions or String Manipulation Functions	147
6.3	Array of Strings or Table of Strings	153
CHAPTER 7	**Functions**	**157**
7.1	Introduction	157
7.2	Function Declaration or Function Prototype	160
7.3	Calling Function and Called Function	160
7.4	Function Call	161
7.5	Return Statement	161

7.6 Function Definition 162
7.7 Actual Arguments and Formal Arguments 163
7.8 Types of Functions Based on Return Value 164
7. 9 Categories of User Defined Functions or Basic Function Design Techniques 165
7.10 Parameter Passing Techniques or Inter function Communication Techniques 171
7.11 Recursion 173
7.12 Storage Classes in C 177

CHAPTER 8 Pointers 183
8.1 Introduction 183
8.2 Basics 183
8.3 Pointer Definition 184
8.4 Declaration 185
8.5 Pointer Initialization 186
8.6 Pointer Expressions 190
8.7 Pointer Arithmetic 191
8.7.1 Pointer Addition and Subtraction 193
8.7.2 Pointer Multiplication and Division 193
8.8 Pointers and Functions 193
8.9 Pointers and Arrays 194
8.9.1 Pointers and One Dimensional Array 194
8.10 Dynamic Memory Allocation (DMA) 196
8.11 Command-Line Arguments 204

CHAPTER 9 Structures and Unions 209
9.1 Introduction 209
9.2 Declaring Structure Variables 210
9.3 Accessing Structure Members 211
9.3.1 Assigning Values to the Members 212
9.3.2 Structure Initialization 212
9.4 Arrays of Structures 216
9.5 Nested Structures 218
9.6 Structures and Functions 221

9.7 Structures and Pointers ... 223
9.8 Self Referential Structures ... 223
9.9 Unions ... 225
9.10 Bit Fields ... 227
9.11 Typedef ... 228
9.12 Enumerations (enum) ... 228

CHAPTER 10 Files ... 231
10.1 Introduction ... 231
10.2 Defining and Opening a File ... 233
10.3 Closing a File ... 237
10.4 File Input and Output Functions ... 237
10.5 Random Access Functions ... 244
10.6 Error Handling Functions ... 248

Glossary ... 251

CHAPTER 1

Introduction to Computers

1.1 Basics

DEFINITION: Computer is an electronic device or machine that capable of doing variety of tasks with speed and accuracy.

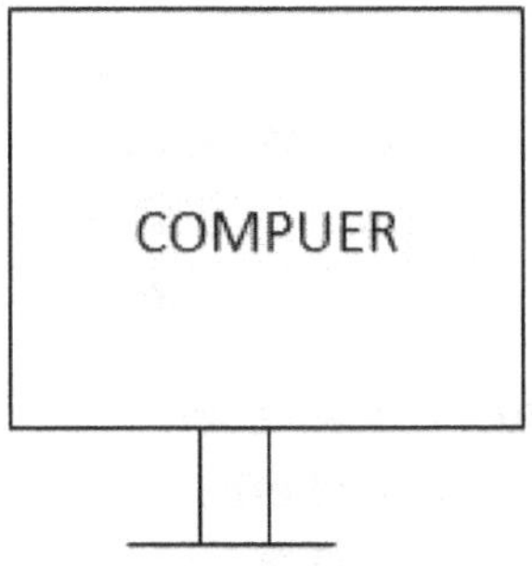

Properties of a Computer:

Speed: computer is an extremely quick machine. It can work big amount of data in a few nano seconds. generally humans worked a meticulous task or tasks for the entire day, electronic machine finishes it by taking very less time. Now a days, very fast computing are there to perform 1000 million calculations very fastly.

electronic machine fastness measured generally as different time units from smallest unit to biggest unit.

s. no	Time unit	Value
1	One second	10^{-12} pico seconds
2	One second	10^{-9} nano seconds
3	One second	10^{-6} micro seconds
4	One second	10^{-3} milli seconds

Accuracy: every time the electronic machines gives the results correctly until unless the user supplies or inputs invalid or incorrect or wrong data. If the user/human gives or inputs or supplies wrong data then the electronic machine or device produces incorrect or wrong results without any doubt. But the machine never does any kind of mistakes during processing the data or performing an operation.

attentiveness: Humans or users have feelings, emotions but not for a computing machine which can hours or days together to work on a data or process te data or performs tasks without deviation in the actual results.

Adaptability: it is one of the best features or characteristics of an electronic machine or machine. It is capable of doing all types or variety of works with speed and accuracy. This is also known as Versatility nature of the computer or computing device.

Memory Capacity: it is also known as storage capacity. user brain can store limited data or information in it where the computer's memory or storage can store big amount of data and that can be takenout on demand.

computerization: based upon the user instructions, the electronic devices do the operation perfectly without deviation in the results.

Iterativeness: The electronic device or computing machine or computer is capable of doing or performing or operating the same task again and again without boring.

confines of a Computing Device:

The imortant confines of a Computing Device are as follows:

Dependability: This machine purely depends on user instructions or commands to do any work or task or performing an operation but can't do anything independently.

No cleverness: As this computing machine has no cleverness or aptitude, it cannot think like a human.

be deficient in identifieng mistakes:

Computing machine is not effective in detecting logical mistakes or wrong calculations.

Poor in decision making:

When the input is given to the comuting device, it cannot validate that data and make a decision as it doesn't have any intelligence.

No way of thinking:

As it's an electronic device, it does not think like human being or user.

MAJOR COMPONENTS OF A COMPUTER

Computing machine or device has two major components or elements

1. Hardware
2. Software

1.1.1 Hardware

The physical components or elements or parts which can be seen and touch by the humans or users are called Hardware.

The hardware consist of the following mainly

a. Cpu
b. Input devices
c. Output devices
d. Storage devices

a) CPU:

The chip or central processing unit or microprocessor is the key element of the computer. Which accepts the data and instructions or commands through input devices, process the data with the help of ALU and that processed data or information will given to the output device as a result or output

CPU has the following elements:

- MU
- ALU
- CU

Memory Unit (MU): its also called Storage Unit. Before starting the manipulation or operation of the facts. The facts and commands that are passed to the computing machine through input devices need to be stored within the computing machine. likewise, the ouputs or answers formed by the computing machine once the manipulation or operation of data is over, those results need to be stored safely with in the computing machine. After that the results can be displayed on output devices.

The main activities are

1. accept the data through input units.
2. store the processed results.
3. display the output through display devices.
4. issue commands to all parts of a computer.

Arithmetic Logic Unit (ALU):

This Arithmetic Logic Unit carries out all the fundamental or primitive arithmetic operations like addition, subtraction, multiplication and division. Also it performs all logical operations like logical OR, logical AND, logical NOT, compelement, rotation, shifting, exclusive OR, comparison of numbers etc. It is answerable for actual completion of commands during manipulation operation. The facts/figures and commands that are with in memory area are moved into Arithmetic

Logic Unit for operation of processing when needed and will be stored back to memory once operation of processing is completed.

once the end of dispensation, the end outputs or results are inside the memory unit before transferred to the output unit. Arithmetic Logic Unit have number of registers which are nothing but mini storage areas. This small area can hold little data and commands which are need to be executed frequently.

functions of Arithmetic Logic Unit are as follows

1. main memory data will be manipulated.
2. addition, subtraction, multiplication and division operations are carried out.
3. all logical operations like logical OR, logical AND, logical NOT, compelement, rotation, shifting, exclusive OR, comparison of numbers etc are performed.

Control Unit(CU): it co ordinates and co operates all the memory unit, Arithmetic Logic Unit, input unit, output unit. It acts like a bridge or mediator among these. It never do any processing or manipulation of data.

Control Unit(CU) functions are:

- It gives instructions to sent the facts/figures through the input unit to memory unit and from memory unit to ALU(Arithmetic Logic Unit).
- It sents the outputs from storage unit to display device.
- It stores the program instructions in storage are, access the instructions one after the another, issues appropriate instructions to the other units of computing machine.
- It fetches the needed program instructions from main memory, interpret it by transferring appropriate commands to the physical unit.

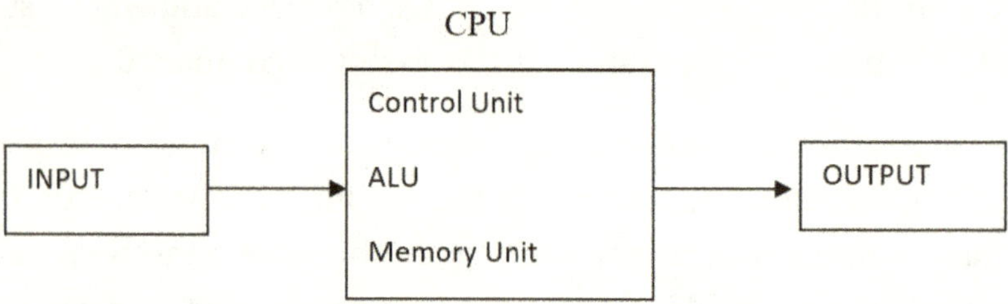

INPUT DEVICES:

Input units act as a medium of communication between the human and the computer which are used to send the data and commands before any operation is carried out.

The most commononly used Input devices are keyboard and mouse.

The other commonly used Input units are micro phone, optical bar code reader, finger print scanner, scanner, web camera, optical mark recognition (OMR), magnetic ink character reader(MICR), punched card, paper tape, Video data entry terminal, joy stick, track ball, touch screen, touch pads, pointing sticks, light pen, etc.

Output units: The Central Processing Unit sends the processed data i. e. information in a human required form on the output unit.

Visual Display Unit, Printer, etc are the most widely used output units or devices.

Visual Display Unit:

Its also called display screen or monitor. when user types some thing on the input unit like keyboard that will be displayed on the screen. user can make corrections if required by looking at the monitor or screen. It's also known as CRT terminal because it uses cathode ray tube inside it. These are available in the form of monochrome which are black and white in color that don't receive any TV signals and color which are clear and sharper because of pixels which are very small points on the screen.

Memory areas:

Memory is also called storage. It is a place where the data, information, commands, instructions of a program stored either temporarily or permanently.

There are different kinds of memory areas or storage devices available.

Registers, Main memory, Cache memory, Auxiliary memory

Registers:

These are also known as internal memory areas where small data stored temporarily and this data is available as long as power supply is available.

Main Memory:

It is also called as primary memory or primary storage device or primary storage area which is available inside the central processing unit or cpu used to store the data, information, values, results for short time. It is a collection of memory cells or locations where data is stored. Each memory location or cell has unique address. Very effectively the data and information can be fetched.

The main memory available in different kinds of form. They are

Random Access Memory(RAM), Read Only Memory(ROM)

RAM is available in different kinds like Dynamic RAM(D RAM), Static RAM(S RAM).

Programmable Read Only Memory(PROM), Erasable Programmable Read Only Memory (EPROM), Elecrically Erasable Erasable Programmable Read Only Memory are also available.

Cache Memory:

This device or storage area is faster than main memory. Compared to main memory it is costlty and tiny device.

The variants of cache are internal cache, external cache.

Auxiliary memory:

Secondary storage area or secondary memory or external memory or external storage device are the different names for auxiliary memory.

Characterstics of auxiliary memory are

- Cheap
- Huge capacity
- Permanent data storage

Different kind of secondary storage devices available are Magnetic tapes, Magnetic disks (Floppy Disk, Hard Disk), Removable storage devices, disk drives, flash drives or memory are best examples for secondary memory.

1.1.2 Software

It is a Program or group of programs intended to perform a specific task or operation or functionality or user requirement. Program is nothing but series of commands or meaningful statements used to perform a specific task or operation or solve a particular problem.

DIFFERENT KINDS OF SOFTWARES:

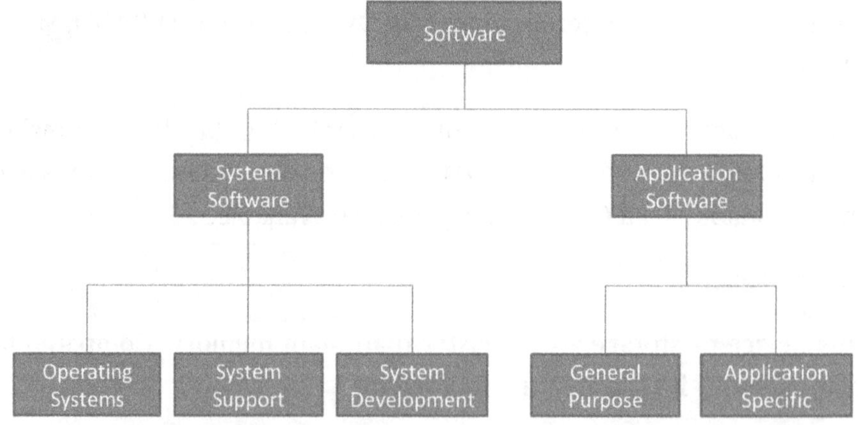

System Software:

This software contains all sub routines or functions in the system memory used to write, execute various application softwares by the user. It acts like an interface between user and different hardware and software components.

Different kinds of system softwares:

Operating System (O. S):

An Operating System is a software or a program intended to execute extra programs on a computer. An operating system is mainly vital software. It is measured as the spine of a computing device organizing various components of software and hardware. It acts like a mediator between hardware and user.

Examples:

UNIX, Linux, DOS, Microsoft windows, Apple's ios, Android, Mac OS.

System support software:

It is also called Utility Software. It is a kind of system software designed to help, analyze, configure, optimize and maintain the computer. A single piece of utility software is usually called a utility or tool.

If we are having any problem related to system then we can solve it through utility software.

For example – Antivirus- Utility scan for computer virus.

The following are the activities those are coming under the utility software are -

- Formatting.
- Backup Recovery.
- Disk Defragmenter.

- Registry Cleaners.
- Disk Partitions. Etc

System development software:

Language Translators: It is a system software converts statements from one language to another language. language to machine level language for the purpose of machine understanding.

There are 3 types of language translator, they are as follows:

- Compiler.
- Interpreter.
- Assembler.

Interpreter	Compiler
Translates program one statement at a time.	Scans the entire program and translates it as a whole into machine code.

Application Software:

Application software products are designed to satisfy a particular need of a particular environment.

General Purpose Application Software:

Software that can be used more than one purpose is called “General Purpose Application Software”.

Examples: Microsoft Notepad, WordPad, MS Word.

Application Specific Software:

This software designed for a Specific Purpose.

Examples: Rail, Bus, hotel, movie tickets reservation systems.

Classification of Computers

The classification of computers is based on the following three categories:-

(1) According to Purpose (2) According to technology used (3) According to size and capacity.

(1) According to Purpose: – According to the utilization of compute for different uses, computers are of following two types:-

i. General Purpose Computers:– Computers that follow instructions for general requirement such as sales analysis, financial accounting, invoicing, inventory, management information etc are called general purpose computers. Almost all computers used in offices for commercial, educational and other applications are general purpose computers.

ii. Special purpose computers:– Computers designed from scratch to perform special tasks like scientific applications and research, weather forecasting, medical diagnostic etc are called special purpose computers.

(2) According to technology used: according to the technology used, computes are of following three types:–

Analog computers: Analog computers are special purpose computers that represent and store data in continuously verifying physical quantities such as current, voltage or frequency. These computers are programmed for measuring physical quantities like temperature, speed etc and to perform computations on these measurements. Analog computers are mainly used for scientific and engineering applications.

Some of the examples of analog computers are given below:–

a) Thermometer:– temperature. It is a simple analog computer used to measure b) Speedometer:– Car's speedometer is another example of analog computer. Where the position of the needle on dial represents the speed of the car.

Digital Computers: Digital computers are mainly general purpose computers that represent and store data in discrete quantities or numbers. In these computers, all processing is done in terms of numeric representation (Binary digits) of data and information. Although the user enters data in decimal or character form, it is converted into binary digits (O's and I's). Almost all the

computers used now days are digital computers.

Hybrid Computers: Hybrid computers combine the technology of both analog and digital computers. These computers store and process analog signals which have been converted into discrete numbers using analog-to- digital converters. They can also convert the digital numbers into analog signals or physical properties using digital to analog converters.

Hybrid computers are faster than analog computers but much slower than digital computers.

It finds applications are special areas.

For example:– In a hospital, analog devices measure the heart functions, temperature and other vital signs of the patients. These measurements are converted into numbers and supplied to a digital computer. This is used to monitor the patient's vital signs and it gives an immediately signal if any abnormal reading is detected.

3) According to size and capacity: According to size and memory/ storage capacity, computers are of following four types:–

Super Computers: Super computers are the biggest and fastest computer, which is mainly designed for complex scientific applications. It has many CPUs (central processing units- main part of computer) which operate in parallel to make it as a fastest computer. These computers are very expensive and more powerful than mainframe computers.

It is typically used fall the following applications:-

- Weatherforecasting
- Petroleum Exploration and production
- Energy Management
- Defense
- Nuclear Energy Research
- Weapons research and development
- Earthquake prediction (seismology)

PARAM and ANURAG are Super Computers produced by India. CRAY3, CRAY-XMP 14, NEC 500, are the another example of supercomputers.

Mainframe Computer: Mainframe computers are very large and fast computers but smaller and slower the super computers. These are used in a centralized location where many terminals (Input/Output devices) are connected with one CPU and thus, allow different users to share the single CPU. They have a very high memory (several hundred megabytes) and can support thousands of users. These computers are faster and more powerful than minicomputers.

They are mainly used for following applications:-

- Railway and Airline Reservations
- Banking Applications
- Commercial Applications of large industries/companies

Some examples of Mainframe Computers are- MEDHA Series, DEC, IBM 3090, IBM 4381, IBM 4300 and IBM ES-9000.

Mini Computer: Minicomputers are medium scale, smaller and generally slower than mainframe computers. Like Mainframes, they have many terminals which are connected with one CPU and can support many users. The cost of minicomputer is very less as compared to mainframe. These computers are faster and more powerful than microcomputers. These computers are suitable for medium class organizations, banks, data processing centers etc.

Some of the examples of minicomputers are PDP-1, IBM AS/400, and DEC MICROVAX, IBM AS/400 is actually a midi computer (computer with performance between a mainframe and minicomputer)is becoming very popular among minicomputers.

Micro Computers: It is a low cost small digital computer. This type of compute contains a microprocessor as its CPU, a memory Unit, Input and Output device. These are also called personal computer system. Maximum speed of micro computers is up to 1 million bytes per second. These types of computers can be used to play games, teach children math, make a painting, create net musical sounds etc.

They are very inexpensive families or home business can afford to buy a small system to use at home.

Micro-Computers can be classified into the following two categories:-

- Desktop Microcomputers
- Portable Micro Computers

Desktop Micro Computers: Common type of Micro Computers, which can easily be accommodated on the top of a desk, is called desktop computers. The usage of such computers is quite common is offices, markets, homes etc.

Portable Micro Computers: These Computers are small is size and looks like a briefcase o a notebook. They are very light in weight and easy to carry from one place to another. They use batteries or electric current.

Examples of these computers are:–

- Laptop Computers
- Notebook Computers

Laptop Computers sometimes called briefcase computes, can be used on your lap and are very portable. Like a desktop computers, laptop computers have a full typewriter keyboard. Laptop computers can be connected to larger peripherals. *Example*: A regular size printer or a large monitor etc.

Notebook Computers are smaller is size than laptop computers. These computers are idle for user who has to wok away from their offices. The users of these computers might be a student, a journalist and a salesman etc.

Example: IBM ThinkPad.

1.2 Computing Environments

What is Computing Environment?

When we want to solve a problem using computer, the computer makes use of various devices which work together to solve that problem. There may be various ways to solve a problem. We use various number of computer devices arranged in different ways to solve different problems. The arrangement of computer devices to solve a problem is said to be computing environment.

The formal definition of computing environment is as follows...

Computing Environment is a collection of computers which are used to process and exchange the information to solve various types of computing problems.

Types of Computing Environments

The following are the various types of computing environments...

1. Personal Computing Environment
2. Time Sharing Computing Environment

3. Client Server Computing Environment
4. Distributed Computing Environment

1. **Personal Computing Environment**

   Personal computing is a standalone machine. In personal computing environment, the complete program resides on standalone machine and executed from the same machine. Laptops, mobile devices, printers, scanners and the computer systems we use at home, office are the examples for personal computing environment.

2. **Time Sharing Computing Environment**

   In this environment users are connected to one or many computers. The user computers are connected to a central computer. The user computers are mini computers and central computer is mainframe computer. There are two shared resources like printers and Disks. These resources are shared by all the user computers.

   The central computer takes main responsibility of managing and controlling the data and printers. Because of this the central computer is always busy and users get slow response from it.

3. **Client Server Computing Environment**

   In this environment, the computing function is divided between user computers and a central computer. The user computers are mini computers and central computer is a mainframe computer. The user computers are called clients and central computer is called a server.

   Work is divided between clients and servers. Because of this client gets fast response from the server and users become more productive.

4. **Distributed Computing Environment**

   The integration of computing function between user computers and servers over a internet is called distributed computing environment.

   In the distributed computing environment, the complete functionality of software is not on single computer but is distributed among multiple computers. Here we use a method of computer processing in which different programs of an application run simultaneously on two or more computers. These computers communicate with each other over a network to perform the complete task. In distributed computing environment, the data is distributed among different systems and that data is logically related to each other

1.3 Computer Languages

What is A Computer Language?

Generally, we use languages like English, Hindi, Telugu etc., to make communication between two persons. That means, when we want to make communication between two persons we need a language through which persons can express their feelings. Similarly, when we want to make communication between user and computer or between two or more computers we need a language through which user can give information to computer. When user wants to give any instruction to the computer the user needs a specific language and that language is known as computer language.

Computer languages are the languages through which user can communicate with the computer by writing program instructions.

Every computer programming language contains a set of predefined words and a set of rules (syntax) that are used to create instructions of a program.

Computer Languages Classification

Over the years, computer languages have been evolved from Low Level to High Level Languages. The computer languages are classified as follows...

1. LOW LEVEL LANGUAGE
2. ASSEMBLY LEVEL LANGUAGE
3. HIGH LEVEL LANGUAGE

Low Level Language (Machine Language)

Low Level language is the only language which can be understood by the computer. **Binary Language** is an example of low level language. Low level language is also known as **Machine Language.** The binary language contains only two symbols 1 & 0. All the instructions of binary language are written in the form of binary numbers 1's & 0's. A computer can directly understand the binary language. Machine language is also known as **Machine Code.**

As the CPU directly understands the binary language instructions, it does not require any translator. CPU directly starts executing the binary language instructions, and takes very less time to execute the instructions as it does not requires any translation. Low level language is considered as the First Generation Language (1GL).

Advantages

- A computer can easily understand the low level language.
- Low level language instructions are executed directly without any translation.
- Low level language instructions require very less time for their execution.

Disadvantages

- Low level language instructions are very difficult to use and understand.
- Low level language instructions are machine dependent, that means a program written for a particular machine does not executes on other machine.
- In low level language, there is more chance for errors and it is very difficult to find errors, debug and modify.

Middle Level Language (Assembly Language)

Middle level language is a computer language in which the instructions are created using symbols such as letters, digits and special characters.. In assembly language, we use predefined words called **mnemonics**. Binary code instructions in low level language are replaced with mnemonics. But computer cannot understand mnemonics, so we use a translator called **Assembler** to translate mnemonics into binary language. Assembler is a translator which takes assembly code as input and produces machine code as output..

Advantages

- Writing instructions in middle level language is easier than writing instructions in low level language.
- Middle level language is more readable compared to low level language.
- Easy to understand, find errors and modify.

Disadvantages

- Middle level language is specific to a particular machine architecture that means it is machine dependent.
- Middle level language needs to be translated into low level language.

- Middle level language executes slower compared to low level language.

High Level Language

- High level language is a computer language which can be understood by the users.
- High level language is very similar to the human languages and has a set of grammar rules that are used to make instructions more easily.
- Every high level language has a set of predefined words known as Keywords and a set of rules known as Syntax to create instructions.
- High level language is easier to understand for the users but the computer cannot understand it.
- High level language needs to be converted into low level language to make it understandable by the computer. We use **Compiler** or **interpreter** to convert high level language to low level language.
- Languages like COBOL, FORTRAN, BASIC, C, C++, JAVA etc., are the examples of high level languages. All these programming languages use human understandable language like English to write program instructions. These instructions are converted to low level language by the compiler so that it can be understood by the computer.

Advantages

- Writing instructions in high level language is easier.
- High level language is more readable and understandable.
- The programs created using high level language runs on different machines with little change or no change.
- Easy to understand, create programs, find errors and modify.

Disadvantages

- High level language needs to be translated to low level language.
- High level language executes slower compared to middle and low level languages.

1.4 Introduction to Problem Solving

1.4.1 Algorithm Development

Definition: it's a step by step process/procedure to solve a problem.

It's a finite set of steps used to solve a problem.

Characteristics:

The algorithm should satisfy the following

1. Input: algorithm should accept or take 0(zero) or more values as input.
2. Output: algorithm should produce at least one value as an output.
3. Finiteness: algorithm should contain finite number of steps.
4. Definiteness: Every step of an algorithm must be clear without any confusion.
5. Effectiveness: The steps of an algorithm can be easily carried out by a person on a paper using pen.

Conventional rules to write an Algorithm

- Every algorithm is enclosed with start (begin), stop (end).
- To accept the data or values from the user, use input or read
- To calculate the result, use compute or calculate.
- To display the message or value, use print or output or display

Ex: 1. To display ranjit, write print " ranjit"

2. To display c value, write print c

Examples for algorithms:

1. Write an algorithm to find sum of two numbers

Ans:

Step 1: start

Step 2: read two numbers a, b

Step 3: calculate c=a+b

Step 4: print c

Step 5: stop

2. Write an algorithm to display your complete name

Ans:

Step 1: start

Step 2: print "My name is M. Anand Ranjit Kumar"

Step 3: stop

3. Write an algorithm to find average of four numbers

Ans:

Step 1: start

Step 2: read four numbers a, b, c, d

Step 3: calculate average = $\frac{a+b+c+d}{4}$

Step 4: print average

Step 5: stop

4. Write an algorithm to find sum, average of four numbers

Ans:

Step 1: start

Step 2: read four numbers a, b, c, d

Step 3: calculate sum = a+b+c+d

Step 4: calculate average = $\frac{\text{sum}}{4}$

Step 5: print sum, average

Step 6: stop

5. Write an algorithm to find simple interest when principal amounts(p), time (t), rate of interest(r) are given.

Ans:

Step 1: start

Step 2: read p, t, and r values

Step 3: calculate simple interest = $\frac{ptr}{100}$

Step 4: print simple interest

Step 5: stop

6. Write an algorithm to find Fahrenheit temperature when Celsius temperature is given.

Ans:

Step 1: start

Step 2: read Celsius temperature say c

Step 3: calculate Fahrenheit temperature say f = $\frac{9 \times c + 32}{100}$

Step 4: print f

Step 5: stop

7. Write an algorithm to find Celsius temperature when Fahrenheit temperature is given.

Ans:

Step 1: start

Step 2: read Fahrenheit temperature say f

Step 3: calculate Celsius temperature say $c = \frac{5\times(f-32)}{9}$

Step 4: print c

Step 5: stop

8. The velocity of an object is given in kilometer/hour. Write an algorithm to convert that velocity into meter/second.

Ans:

Step 1: start

Step 2: read velocity in kilometer/hour say vkh

Step 3: calculate velocity in meter/second say $vms = \frac{5 \times vkh}{18}$

Step 4: print c

Step 5: stop

9. Write an algorithm to find sum of n natural numbers

Ans:

Step 1: start

Step 2: read n value

Step 3: calculate $sum = \frac{n \times (n+1)}{2}$

Step 4: print sum

Step 5: stop

10. Write an algorithm to find sum of cubes of n natural numbers i. e. $1^3+2^3+3^3+$.....

Ans:

Step 1: start

Step 2: read n value

Step 3: calculate sum= $\frac{n^2 \times (n+1)^2}{4}$

Step 4: print sum

Step 5: stop

Exercise:

- Write an algorithm to find area, perimeter of a rectangle.
- Write an algorithm to find area, perimeter of a circle.
- Write an algorithm to find area, perimeter of a triangle.
- Write an algorithm to find area of a cuboid.
- Write an algorithm to find area of a cone.
- Write an algorithm to calculate sum, difference, multiplication and division of two numbers and display the results.
- Write an algorithm to find sum of squares of n natural numbers.
- Write an algorithm to find volume of cylinder (hint: volume = $\pi r^2 h$)
- Write an algorithm to find volume of sphere (hint: volume= $\frac{4\pi r^3}{3}$)
- Write an algorithm to find volume of Cone (hint: volume= $\frac{\pi r^2 h}{3}$)

1.4.2 Flowchart

1. Graphical representation of any program is called flowchart.
2. There are some standard graphics that are used in flowchart as following:

Flow chart Symbols

s.no	Symbol name	symbol	use
1	Start/Stop terminal box		Indicates starting/ ending of a process or an algorithm
2	Input/Output box		Input or output purpose
3	Process/ Instruction box		Statement or instruction writing.
4	Lines or Arrows		Connecting the flow chart symbols
5	Decision box		It's also called condition symbol which can be either true or false
6	connector		To connect the parts of a flow chart
7	loop		For repetition purpose
8	Sub program		Sub function or module
9	cylinder		Secondary storage device

1. Draw a flowchart to find lcm

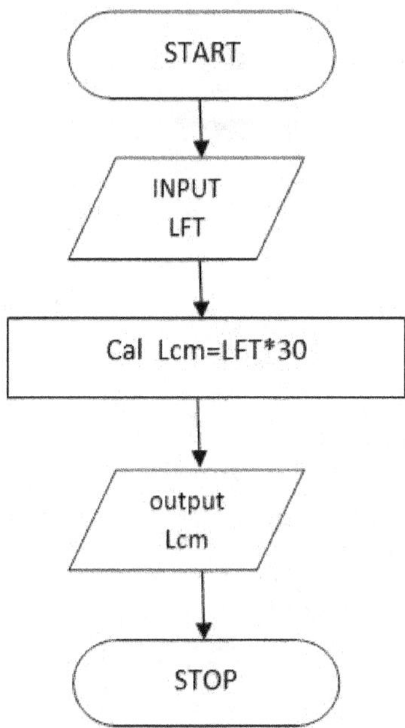

2. Draw a flowchart that will read the two sides of a rectangle and calculate its area.

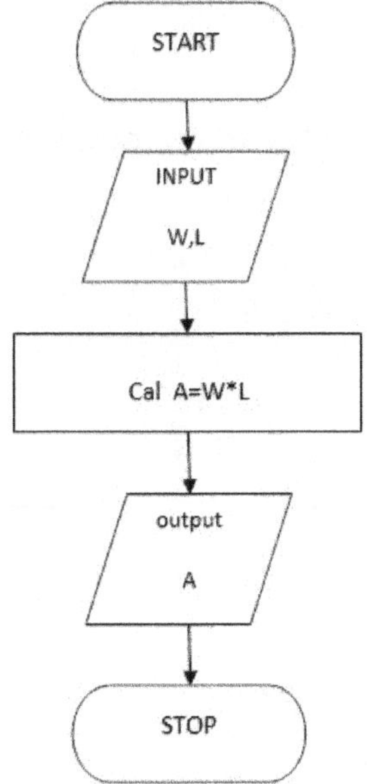

3. Draw a flowchart that will calculate the roots of a quadratic equation

START

INPUT

Cal d=b²-4ac

d>=0?

True

false

Cal r1=(-b+√d)/(2*a)

r2=(-b-√d)/(2*a)

Cal r1=(-b+√-d)/(2*a)

r2=(-b-√-d)/(2*a)

ouput

r1,r2 values

STOP

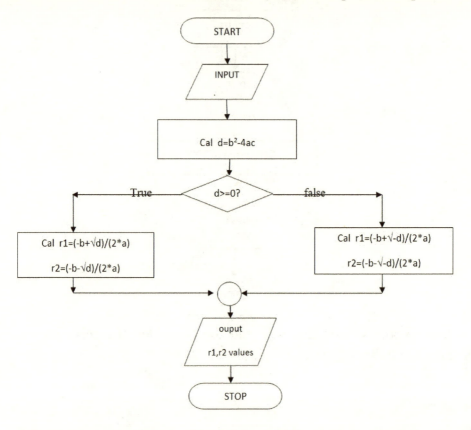

4. Draw a flowchart to read the temperature and display the message.

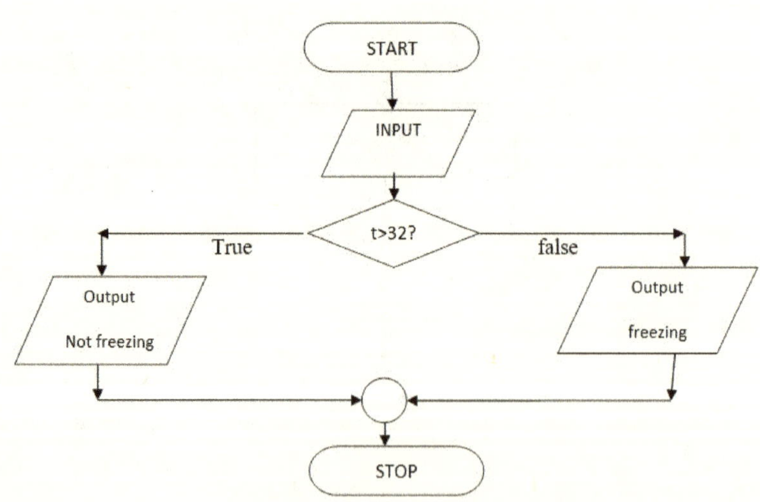

Exercise:

1. Draw a flowchart to find area, perimeter of a rectangle.
2. Draw a flowchart to find area, perimeter of a circle.
3. Draw a flowchart to find area, perimeter of a triangle.
4. Draw a flowchart to find area of a cuboid.
5. Draw a flowchart to find area of a cone.
6. Draw a flowchart to calculate sum, difference, multiplication and division of two numbers and display the results.
7. Draw a flowchart to find sum of squares of n natural numbers.
8. Draw a flowchart to find volume of cylinder (hint: volume = $\pi r^2 h$)
9. Draw a flowchart to find volume of sphere (hint: volume = $\frac{4\pi r^3}{3}$)
10. Draw a flowchart to find volume of Cone (hint: volume= $\frac{\pi r^{2h}}{3}$)

Pseudo code:

It is an artificial and informal language to write an algorithm.

1.5 Program Development Life Cycle (or) Software Development Life Cycle (SDLC)

Computer is an Electronic Device that can do variety of tasks based on user instructions. The user has to instruct the computer what it supposed to do in a form which a computer can understand.

To make communication with the computers we write programs using computer languages. Program is nothing but set of instructions.

To develop a good program/software to solve a problem, we need to follow some steps. These steps are called PROGRAM DEVELOPMENT

STEPS (OR) PROGRAM DEVELOPMENT LIFE CYCLE (OR) SOFTWARE DEVELOPMENT LIFE CYCLE (SDLC).

The steps are

1. Feasibility Study
2. Requirement Analysis
3. Design
4. Coding
5. Debugging and Testing
6. Deployment
7. Documentation & Maintenance

1. Feasibility Study:

In this step, we understand the problem clearly by reading and re reading and then we decide whether that problem can be solvable on a computer or not. After this step only the remaining steps are carried out.

2. Requirement Analysis:

In this step, we identify the values (input) that required for solving the problem, software requirements (which operating system, languages... etc. we have to use to develop a program), Hardware Requirements (Specifies which processor, how much memory is required).

3. Design:

In this step, we write an Algorithm to solve the problem.

Algorithm is a step by step process to solve the problem.

4. Coding:

In this step, we write the program according to an algorithm using one of the computer programming languages. We can use c, c++, java.

5. Debugging and Testing:

Debugging means checking whether our written program is correct or not according to language rules. If not, we make our program correct by modifying the statements in the program.

Testing means we test our program by giving some values as input and verify whether our program is giving correct results or not. If not, we make some changes in the program.

6. Deployment:

In this step, we install the system in the customer's site or we release the developed software in the market.

7. Documentation and Maintenance:

Documentation helps the user to understand, use and follow the software or program easily.

Maintenance keeps the system up to date according to user requirements.

CHAPTER 2

Introduction to C Programming

2.1 History

- C is a programming language which born at "AT&T's Bell Laboratory" of USA in 1972.
- C was written by Dennis Ritchie, that's why he is also called as father of c programming language.
- C language was created for a specific purpose i. e. designing the UNIX operating system (which is currently base of many UNIX based OS).
- From the beginning, C was intended to be useful to allow busy programmers to get things done because C is such a powerful, dominant and supple language
- Its use quickly spread beyond Bell Labs in the late 70's because of its long list of strong features
- Why Name "C" was given to Language ?
- Many of C's principles and ideas were derived from the earlier language B. (Ken Thompson was the developer of B Language.)
- BCPL and CPL are the earlier ancestors of B Language

- CPL is common Programming Language. In 1967, BCPL Language (Basic CPL) was created as a scaled down version of CPL
- As many of the **features were derived from "B" Language that's why it was named as "C".**
- After 7-8 years C++ came into existence which was first example of object oriented programming.

Time streak of Programming Language C:

Language Name	Invented in the Year	Invented by
ALGOL	1960	International Group
Basic Combined Programming Language	1967	Martin Richards
B	1970	Ken Thompson
C or Traditional C	1972	Dennis Ritchie
K&R C	1978	Brian Kernighan and Dennis Ritchie
ANSI C	1989	ANSI Committee
ISO C	1990	ISO Committee

C Character Set:

Whenever we write any C program then it consists of different statements. Each C Program is set of statements and each statement is set of different c programming lexims. In C Programming each and every character is considered as single lexim. i.e [Basic Lexical Element]

Character Set Consists Of C

Types	Character Set
Lowercase Letters	a-z
Uppercase Letters	A to Z
Digits	0-9
Special Characters	!@#$%^&*.. etc
White Spaces	Tab Or New line Or Space

Valid C Characters:

Special Characters are listed below

<table>
<tr><th>Symbol</th><th>Meaning</th></tr>
<tr><td>*</td><td>Asterisk</td></tr>
<tr><td>&</td><td>Ampersand</td></tr>
<tr><td>#</td><td>Number sign</td></tr>
<tr><td>$</td><td>Dollar sign</td></tr>
<tr><td>%</td><td>Percent sign</td></tr>
<tr><td>^</td><td>Caret</td></tr>
<tr><td>!</td><td>Exclamation mark</td></tr>
<tr><td>~</td><td>Tilde</td></tr>
<tr><td>(</td><td>Left parenthesis</td></tr>
<tr><td>)</td><td>Right parenthesis</td></tr>
<tr><td>_</td><td>Underscore</td></tr>
<tr><td>+</td><td>Plus sign</td></tr>
<tr><td>|</td><td>Vertical bar</td></tr>
<tr><td>\</td><td>Backslash</td></tr>
<tr><td>`</td><td>Apostrophe</td></tr>
<tr><td>–</td><td>Minus sign</td></tr>
<tr><td>=</td><td>Equal to sign</td></tr>
<tr><td>{</td><td>Left brace</td></tr>
<tr><td>}</td><td>Right brace</td></tr>
</table>

Continued...

[	Left bracket
]	Right bracket
:	Colon
”	Quotation mark
;	Semicolon
<	Opening angle bracket
>	Closing angle bracket
?	Question mark
,	Comma
.	Period
/	Slash

2.2 C Tokens

- C tokens are the basic buildings blocks in C language which are constructed together to write a C program.
- Each and every smallest individual units in a C program are known as C tokens.

C tokens are of six types. They are,

1. Keywords (eg: int, while),
2. Identifiers (eg: main, total),
3. Constants (eg: 10, 20),
4. Strings (eg: “total”, “hello”),
5. Special symbols (eg: (), {}),
6. Operators (eg: +,/,-,*)

Constants/Literals

A constant is a value or an identifier whose value cannot be altered in a program. For example: 1, 2. 5, “C programming is easy”, etc.

Types of C constants:

1. Integer constants
2. Real or Floating point constants
3. Character constants
4. Backslash or Escape sequence character constants
5. String constants

1. Integer constants

An integer constant is a numeric constant (associated with number) without any fractional or exponential part. There are three types of integer constants in C programming:

- decimal constant(base 10)
- octal constant(base 8)
- hexadecimal constant(base 16)

For example:

Decimal constants: 0, -9, 22 etc

Octal constants: 021, 077, 033 etc

Hexadecimal constants: 0x7f, 0x2a, 0x521 etc

In C programming, octal constant starts with a 0 and hexadecimal constant starts with a 0X or oX

2. Floating-point constants

A floating point constant is a numeric constant that has either a fractional form or an exponent form. For example:

-2. 0

0. 0000234

-0. 22E-5

Note: E-5 = 10^{-5}

3. Character constants

A character constant is a constant which uses single quotation around characters. For example: 'a', 'l', 'm', 'F'

4. Escape Sequences (non printable characters)

Sometimes, it is necessary to use characters which cannot be typed or has special meaning in C programming. For example: newline(enter), tab, question mark etc. In order to use these characters, escape sequence is used.

For example: \n is used for newline. The backslash (\) causes "escape" from the normal way the characters are interpreted by the compiler.

Escape Sequences	
Escape Sequences	Character
\b	Backspace
\f	Form feed
\n	Newline
\r	Return
\t	Horizontal tab
\v	Vertical tab
\\	Backslash
\'	Single quotation mark
\"	Double quotation mark
\?	Question mark
\0	Null character

5. String constants

String constants are the constants which are enclosed in a pair of double-quote marks. For example:

```
"good"          //string constant
""      //null string constant
"      "        //string constant of six white space
"x"     //string constant having single character.
"Earth is round\n"      //prints string with newline
```

VARIABLES

Definition:

- **Variable is a name used to store or hold a constant.**
- C variable is a named location in a memory where a program can manipulate the data. This location is used to hold the value of the variable.
- The value of the C variable may get change in the program.
- C variable might be belonging to any of the data type like int, float, char etc.

RULES FOR NAMING C VARIABLE:

1. Variable name must begin with letter or underscore.
2. Variables are case sensitive
3. They can be constructed with digits, letters.
4. No special symbols are allowed other than underscore.
5. sum, height, _value are some examples for variable name
6. 9sum, sum of four numbers, &abc are invalid variables.

2.3 Key Words

Keywords are pre defined, reserved words used in programming that have special meanings to the compiler. Keywords are part of the syntax and they cannot be used as an identifier.

For example: int money;

Here, int is a keyword that indicates 'money' is a variable of type integer.

As C is a case sensitive language, all keywords must be written in lowercase. Here is a list of all keywords allowed in ANSI C.

Keywords in C Language			
auto	double	int	struct
break	else	long	switch
case	enum	register	typedef
char	extern	return	union
continue	for	signed	void
do	if	static	while
default	goto	sizeof	volatile
const	float	short	unsigned

Along with these keywords, C supports other numerous keywords depending upon the compiler.

C Identifiers

Identifier refers to name given to entities such as variables, functions, structures etc.

Identifier must be unique. They are created to give unique name to a entity to identify it during the execution of the program. For example:

int money;

double account_Balance;

Here, money and account_Balance are identifiers.

Also remember, identifier names must be different from keywords. You cannot use int as an identifier because int is a keyword.

Rules for writing an identifier

1. A valid identifier can have letters (both uppercase and lowercase letters), digits and underscores.

2. The first letter of an identifier should be either a letter or an underscore. However, it is discouraged to start an identifier name with an underscore.

3. There is no rule on length of an identifier. However, the first 31 characters of identifiers are discriminated by the compiler.

2.4 Data Types in C

Data types specify how we enter data into our programs and what type of data we enter. C language has some predefined set of data types to handle various kinds of data that we use in our program. These data types have different storage capacities.

C language supports 3 different type of data types,

Primary data types or Basic or primitive or Fundamental

These are fundamental data types in C namely integer(**int**), floating(**float**), character(**char**) and **void**.

Derived data types

These are derived from the basic or fundamental or primitive datatypes. Derived data types are like array, function and pointer.

User Defined data types: These are created or defined by the user. examples: structures, unions, enumerators.

Integer type

Integers are used to store whole numbers.

Size and range of Integer type on 16-bit machine

Data Type	Size(in bytes)	Range of values
int or signed int	2	-32768 to 32767
unsigned int	2	0 to 65535
short int or signed short int	1	-128 to 127
unsigned short int	1	0 to 255
long int or signed long int	4	-2147483648 to 2147483, 647
unsigned long int	4	0 to 4294967295

Floating type

Floating types are used to store real numbers.

Size and range of Integer type on 16-bit machine

Data Type	Size(in bytes)	Range of values
Float	4	3. 4E-38 to 3. 4E+38
Double	8	1. 7E-308 to 1. 7E+308
long double	10	3. 4E-4932 to 1. 1E+4932

Character type

Character types are used to store characters value.

Size and range of Integer type on 16-bit machine

Type	Size(bytes)	Range
char or signed char	1	-128 to 127
unsigned char	1	0 to 255

void type

void type means no value. This is usually used to specify the type of functions.

2.5 Different Statements

By combining constants, variables, keywords, identifiers, we can write statements like declaration statement, input and output statement.

1. Declaration Statement:

We must write or declare the variables before they are used in the program.

Syntax:

Datatype variable(s);

Examples: 1. int a;

float b;

char c;

Here a, b, c are variables and int, float, char are datatypes.

2. More than one variables are separated by comma (,)

Examples: int a, b, c;

char x, y;

float p, q, r;

2. Formatted input and output statements:

Formatted input:

In C, scanf () is called formatted input function/statement used to give (read) the values to the variables during execution of the program.

Syntax:

scanf(" control string ", &variable1,&variable2,...);

1. In control string, we write %d,%c,%f for integer, character and float type variables.

2. & gives the address. variable gives the address of a variable which tells the compiler where the entered value to be stored.

Examples:

1. int a, b, c;

To read values for a, b, c

scanf(“%d%d%d”,&a,&b,&c);

2. int a;

float b;

char c;

To read/enter values for a, b, c

scanf(“%d%f%c”,&a,&b,&c);

3. float a, b, c;

To read values for a, b, c

scanf (“%f%f%f”,&a,&b,&c);

Formatted output:

In C, printf () is called formatted output function/statement used to display (print) the values of the variables during execution of the program.

Syntax:

printf(“control string ”, variable1, variable2,...);

- In control string, we write %d,%c,%f for integer, character and float type variables.
- When we want to print only text that text to be written in “ “ only.

Example:

To print "welcome to c"

printf("welcome to c");

- To print the values of various variables, we can write printf() in one of the following ways

Example:

Int a; float b; char c;

Assume a=10, b=5. 123, c='$'

To print a, b, c values output

printf("%d%f%c", a, b, c); 105. 123000$

- To print a, b, c values output

printf("%d %f %c", a, b, c); 10 5. 123000 $

- To print a, b, c values output

printf("a value=%d \n b value=%f \n c value=%c", a, b, c); a value=10

b value=5. 123000 c value=$

2.6 Structure of a C program

The Structure of a C program contains the following sections.

Documentation/comments Section
Linking or inlcude Section
Definition Section
Global Declaration Section

void main() function section
{
Declaration part
Executable part
}

Continued...

```
Subprogram/userdefined functions section
Function1( )
{
}
Function2( )
{
}
----------
----------
Function n( )
{
}
```

1. Documentation section: The documentation section consists of a set of comment lines giving the name of the program, the author and other details, which the programmer would like to use later.

2. Link section: The link section provides instructions to the compiler to link functions from the system library such as using the #include directive.

3. Definition section: The definition section defines all symbolic constants such using the #define directive.

4. Global declaration section: There are some variables that are used in more than one function. Such variables are called global variables and are declared in the global declaration section that is outside of all the functions. This section also declares all the user-defined functions.

5. main () function section: Every C program must have one main function section. This section contains two parts; declaration part and executable part. These two parts must appear between the opening and closing braces. The program execution begins

at the opening brace and ends at the closing brace. The closing brace of the main function is the logical end of the program.

1. Declaration part: The declaration part declares all the variables used in the executable part.
2. Executable part: There is at least one statement in the executable part.

All statements in the declaration and executable part end with a semicolon.

1. Subprogram section: If the program is a multi-function program then the subprogram section contains all the user-defined functions that are called in the main () function. User-defined functions are generally placed immediately after the main () function, although they may appear in any order.

Note:

All section, except the main () function section may be absent(optional) when they are not required.

2.7 Creating and Running a C Program

Creating and running of a c program contains the following steps

1. Writing and modifying the C program
2. Compiling the C program
3. Linking the C program
4. Executing the C program.

1. Writing and modifying the C program:

User can type or write the program in a software called editor. notepad, wordpad, gedit are examples for editors. After writing the program the user saves the program. This saved program is called source program or source file. Every c program has an extension. c

Example: gedit sum. c

This command used to open the editor. Here sum. c is the source program.

2. Compiling the C program:

After saving the program, user compiles the program. In the compilation, the source program is converted in to machine language instructions (0's and 1's) and this converted file is called object file (Example: sum. obj) when there are no mistakes in the program. If mistakes or errors are there in the program, then the compiler gives error messages. To correct the errors or mistakes, we go to editor and modify or change program statements.

Example: gcc sum. c

This is the command for compilation.

3. Linking the C program:

In this Linker links the functions from header file or system library with object file and generates a file called executable file Example: sum. exe). The contents of executable file are in 0's and 1's. if mistakes or errors are there in the program, then we get error messages. To correct the errors or mistakes, we go to editor and modify or change program statements.

4. Executing the C program:

User executes the program using ./a. out command to see the output or result of the written program. if the output or result of the program is wrong, then we go to editor and modify or change program statements.

Example: ./a. out

CHAPTER 3

Operators in C

3.1 Introduction

An operator is a symbol that tells the compiler to perform specific mathematical or logical functions. C language is rich in built-in operators and provides the following types of operators –

- Arithmetic Operators
- Relational Operators
- Logical Operators
- Bitwise Operators
- Increment/decrement operators
- Conditional operators
- Assignment Operators
- Special Operators

1. Arithmetic Operators

The following table shows all the arithmetic operators supported by the C language. Assume variable **P** holds 10 and variable **Q** holds 20 then –

Operator	Description	Example
+	Adds two operands.	P + Q = 30
–	Subtracts second operand from the first operand.	P – Q = -10
*	Multiplies both operands.	P * Q = 200
/	Divides numerator by de-numerator which gives quotient values of the division operation	Q/ P = 2
%	Modulus division Operator and remainder value after an integer division.	Q % P = 0

2. Relational Operators

The following table shows all the relational operators supported by C. Assume variable **P** holds 10 and variable **Q** holds 20 then –

Operator	Description	Example
==	Checks if the values of two operands are equal or not. If yes, then the condition becomes true(1) otherwise false(0)..	(P == Q) is not true.
!=	Checks if the values of two operands are equal or not. If the values are not equal, then the condition becomes true(1) otherwise false(0).	(P != Q) is true.
>	Checks if the value of left operand is greater than the value of right operand. If yes, then the condition becomes true(1) otherwise false(0)..	(P > Q) is not true.
<	Checks if the value of left operand is less than the value of right operand. If yes, then the condition becomes true(1) otherwise false(0)..	(P < Q) is true.

>=	Checks if the value of left operand is greater than or equal to the value of right operand. If yes, then the condition becomes true(1) otherwise false(0)..	(P >= Q) is not true.
<=	Checks if the value of left operand is less than or equal to the value of right operand. If yes, then the condition becomes true(1) otherwise false(0)..	(P <= Q) is true.

3. Logical Operators

Following table shows all the logical operators supported by C language. Assume variable **P** holds 1 and variable **Q** holds 0, then –

<table>
<tr><th>Operator</th><th>Description</th><th>Example</th></tr>
<tr><td>&&</td><td>Called Logical AND operator. If both the operands are non-zero, then the condition becomes true(1) otherwise false(0).</td><td>(P && Q) is false(0).</td></tr>
<tr><td>||</td><td>Called Logical OR Operator. If any of the two operands is non-zero, then the condition becomes true(1) otherwise false(0).</td><td>(P || Q) is true(1).</td></tr>
<tr><td>!</td><td>Called Logical NOT Operator. It is used to reverse the logical state of its operand. If a condition is true, then Logical NOT operator will make it false.</td><td>!(P && Q) is true(1).</td></tr>
</table>

4. Bitwise Operators

Bitwise operator works on bits and perform bit-by-bit operation. The truth tables for &, |, and ^ is as follows –

p	q	p & q	p | q	p ^ q
0	0	0	0	0
0	1	0	1	1
1	1	1	1	0
1	0	0	1	1

Assume A = 60 and B = 13 in binary format, they will be as follows –

A = 0011 1100

B = 0000 1101

A&B = 0000 1100

A|B = 0011 1101

A^B = 0011 0001

~A = 1100 0011

The following table lists the bitwise operators supported by C. Assume variable P holds 60 and variable Q holds 13, then

Operator	Description	Example
&	Binary AND Operator gives 1 if it exists in both operands otherwise 0	(P & Q) = 12, i. e., 0000 1100
|	Binary OR Operator gives 1 if it exists in any one of the operands otherwise 0	(P | Q) = 61, i. e., 0011 1101
^	Binary XOR Operator gives 1 if both bits are different otherwise 0	(P ^ Q) = 49, i. e., 0011 0001

~	Binary Ones Complement Operator is unary and has the effect of 'flipping' bits or converting 1 to 0 and vice versa.	(~P) = -61, i. e,. 1100 0011 in 2's complement form.
<<	Binary Left Shift Operator. The left operands value is moved left by the number of bits specified by the right operand.	P << 2 = 240 i. e., 1111 0000
>>	Binary Right Shift Operator. The left operands value is moved right by the number of bits specified by the right operand.	P >> 2 = 15 i. e., 0000 1111

Note: Remember the following

1. ~n=-(n+1)
2. **A<<B** is equal to **A * 2^B**
3. **A>>B** is equal to **A/ 2^B**

5. Increment and decrement operators

C programming has two operators increment ++ and decrement -- to change the value of an operand (variable) by 1.

Increment ++ increases the value by 1 whereas decrement -- decreases the value by 1. These two operators are unary operators, meaning they only operate on a single operand.

Increment operator (++): There are two types of increment operators

a. Pre Increment operator: if the increment operator (++) exists in the left side of operand then it is called pre increment operator.

   Ex: ++a

   ++a is equal to a=a+1

   When increment operator present in the expression, first the value of variable icreases by 1, later that value used in the expression.

   Ex: x=5;

   y=++x;

   This expression equals to

   x=x+1 i. e. x=5+1, x=6

   And y=x i. e. y=6

b. Post Increment operator: if the increment operator (++) exists in the right side of operand then it is called post increment operator.

   Ex: a++

   a++ is equal to a=a+1

   When increment operator present in the expression, first the value of variable used in the expression later it increases by 1.

   Ex: x=5;

   y=x++;

   This expression equals to

   y=x i. e. y=5

   and x=x+1 i. e. x=5+1, x=6

Decrement operator (--): There are two types of decrement operators

a. Pre decrement operator: if the increment operator (--) exists in the left side of operand then it is called pre decrement operator.

   Ex: --a

   --a is equal to a=a-1

   When decrement operator present in the expression, first the value of variable decreases by 1, later that value used in the expression.

   Ex: x=5;

   y=--x;

   This expression equals to

   x=x-1 i. e. x=5-1, x=4

   And y=x i. e. y=4

b. Post decrement operator: if the decrement operator (--) exists in the right side of operand then it is called post decrement operator.

   Ex: a--

   a-- is equal to a=a-1

   When decrement operator present in the expression, first the value of variable used in the expression later it decreases by 1.

   Ex: x=5;

   y=x--;

   This expression equals to

   y=x i. e. y=5

   and x=x-1 i. e. x=5-1, x=4

Example:

```
// C Program to demonstrate the working of increment and decrement operators

#include <stdio. h>

int main()

{

        int a = 101, b = 1001;

        float c = 100. 5, d = 1000. 5;

        printf("++a = %d \n", ++a);

        printf("--b = %d \n", --b);

        printf("++c = %f \n", ++c);

        printf("--d = %f \n", --d);

        return 0;

}
```

Output

```
++a = 102

--b = 1000

++c = 101. 500000

++d = 999. 500000
```

6. Assignment Operators

The following table lists the assignment operators supported by the C language

Operator	Description	Example
=	Simple assignment operator. Assigns values from right side operands to left side operand	C = A + B will assign the value of A + B to C
+=	Add assignment operator. It adds the right operand to the left operand and assigns the result to the left operand.	C += A is equivalent to C = C + A
-=	Subtract assignment operator. It subtracts the right operand from the left operand and assigns the result to the left operand.	C -= A is equivalent to C = C - A
*=	Multiply assignment operator. It multiplies the right operand with the left operand and assigns the result to the left operand.	C *= A is equivalent to C = C * A
/=	Divide assignment operator. It divides the left operand with the right operand and assigns the result to the left operand.	C/= A is equivalent to C = C/A
%=	Modulus assignment operator. It takes modulus using two operands and assigns the result to the left operand.	C %= A is equivalent to C = C % A
<<=	Left shift and assignment operator.	C <<= 2 is same as C = C << 2
>>=	Right shift and assignment operator.	C >>= 2 is same as C = C >> 2
&=	Bitwise and assignment operator.	C &= 2 is same as C = C & 2
^=	Bitwise exclusive OR and assignment operator.	C ^= 2 is same as C = C ^ 2

Continued...

|=	Bitwise inclusive OR and assignment operator.	C |= 2 is same as C = C | 2

7. C Ternary Operator (?:)

A conditional operator is a ternary operator, that is, it works on 3 operands.

Conditional Operator Syntax

conditionalExpression ? expression1: expression2

The conditional operator works as follows:

- The first expression conditionalExpression is evaluated first. This expression evaluates to 1 if it's true and evaluates to 0 if it's false.
- If conditionalExpression is true, expression1 is evaluated.
- If conditionalExpression is false, expression2 is evaluated.

Example: C conditional Operator

```
#include <stdio. h>

int main(){

    char February;

    int days;

    printf("If this year is leap year, enter 1. If not enter any integer: ");

    scanf("%c",&February);


    // If test condition (February == 'l') is true, days equal to 29.

    // If test condition (February =='l') is false, days equal to 28.

    days = (February == '1') ? 29: 28;
```

```
    printf("Number of days in February = %d", days);
    return 0;
}
```

Output

If this year is leap year, enter 1. If not enter any integer: 1

Number of days in February = 29

8. Special Operators: sizeof & *,

Besides the operators discussed above, there are a few other important operators including **sizeof** and **& ***, supported by the C Language.

Operator	**Description**	**Example**
sizeof()	Returns the size of a variable.	sizeof(a), where a is integer, will return 2.
&	Returns the address of a variable.	&a; returns the actual address of the variable.
*	Pointer to a variable.	*a;
,	Used to join the expressions	int a, b, c;

3.2 Operators Precedence in C

Operator precedence determines the grouping of terms in an expression and decides how an expression is evaluated. Certain operators have higher precedence than others; for example, the multiplication operator has a higher precedence than the addition operator.

For example, x = 7 + 3 * 2; here, x is assigned 13, not 20 because operator * has a higher precedence than +, so it first gets multiplied with 3*2 and then adds into 7.

Here, operators with the highest precedence appear at the top of the table, those with the lowest appear at the bottom. Within an expression, higher precedence operators will be evaluated first.

<table>
<tr><th>Category</th><th>Operator</th><th>Associativity</th></tr>
<tr><td>Postfix</td><td>() [] ->. ++ - -</td><td>Left to right</td></tr>
<tr><td>Unary</td><td>+ - ! ~ ++ - - (type)* & sizeof</td><td>**Right to left**</td></tr>
<tr><td>Multiplicative</td><td>*/%</td><td>Left to right</td></tr>
<tr><td>Additive</td><td>+ -</td><td>Left to right</td></tr>
<tr><td>Shift</td><td><< >></td><td>Left to right</td></tr>
<tr><td>Relational</td><td>< <= > >=</td><td>Left to right</td></tr>
<tr><td>Equality</td><td>== !=</td><td>Left to right</td></tr>
<tr><td>Bitwise AND</td><td>&</td><td>Left to right</td></tr>
<tr><td>Bitwise XOR</td><td>^</td><td>Left to right</td></tr>
<tr><td>Bitwise OR</td><td>|</td><td>Left to right</td></tr>
<tr><td>Logical AND</td><td>&&</td><td>Left to right</td></tr>
<tr><td>Logical OR</td><td>||</td><td>Left to right</td></tr>
<tr><td>Conditional</td><td>?:</td><td>**Right to left**</td></tr>
<tr><td>Assignment</td><td>= += -= *=/= %=>>= <<= &= ^= |=</td><td>**Right to left**</td></tr>
<tr><td>Comma</td><td>,</td><td>Left to right</td></tr>
</table>

3.3 Expressions and it's Evaluation

An expression is a combination of variables constants and operators written according to the syntax of C language. In C every expression evaluates to a value i. e., every expression results in some value of a certain type that can be assigned to a variable. Some examples of C expressions are shown in the table given below.

Algebraic Expression	C Expression
a x b – c	a * b – c
(m + n) (x + y)	(m + n) * (x + y)
(ab/c)	a * b/c
$3x^2$ +2x + 1	3*x*x+2*x+1
(x/y) + c	x/y + c

Expressions Evaluation:

In C programming language, expression is evaluated based on the operator precedence and associativity. When there are multiple operators in an expression, they are evaluated according to their precedence and associativity. The operator with higher precedence is evaluated first and the operator with least precedence is evaluated last.

An expression is evaluated based on the precedence and associativity of the operators in that expression.

To understand expression evaluation in C, let us consider the following simple example expression...

10 + 4 * 3/2

In the above expression there are three operators +, * **and/**. Among these three operators, both multiplication and division have same higher precedence and addition has lower precedence. So, according to the operator precedence both multiplication and division are evaluated first and then addition is evaluated. As multiplication and division have same precedence they are evaluated based on the associativity. Here, the associativity of multiplication and division is **left to right**. So, multiplication is performed first, then division and finally addition. So, the above expression is evaluated in the order of */**and** +. It is evaluated as follows...

4 * 3 ====> 12
12/2 ===> 6
10 + 6 ===> 16

the expression is evaluated to **16.**

Example 1: Using expressions

Consider the code

a = b += c++ – d + ––e/–f ;

Highest precedence is for c++ Next in precedence order are: --e and -f

So putting parentheses in that order around the expressions:

a = b += **(c++)** – d + **(––e)/(– f)** ;

And finally, full parenthetic expression will be

(a = (b += (((c++) – d) + ((––e)/(– f)))));

With a=1, b=2, c=12, d=2, e=5, f=2, it evaluates: a = 10, b = 10

Example 2:

- -a + (c + b * (c + a)/c - b/a) + a - b/2

will be evaluated as

(((-a) + ((c + ((b * (c + a))/c)) - (b/a))) - (b/2))

Example 3:

- Assume int i = 5, j = 10, k = 2, result;

Then value result = 2 * i % 5 * 4 + (j - 3)/(k + 2);

will be evaluated as

((((2*i)%5) * 4) + ((j-3)/(k+2))) which is 0

- Whereas result = 2 * i % (5 * 4) + (j - 3)/(k + 2); evaluated as 11

Example 4:

```
int main ( )
{
        int i ;
        printf ("Enter a two digit number:");
        scanf ("%d", &i);
printf ("reversed number is: %d\n ", i %10*10 + i/10);
return 0;
}
```

Exercise:

1. Determine the following expressions values, when x=8, y=9

   a. x&y
   b. x|y
   c. x^y
   d. ~x
   e. x<<4
   f. y>>1

2. Determine the following expressions values.

   Int i=8, j=5, k;
   Float x=0. 005, y=-0. 01, z;
   Char a, b, c='d', d='c';

   - i-=(j>0)?j: 0;
   - a=(y>=0)y: 0;
   - i+=(j-2);
   - z=(j==5)?i: j;

3. x=4, what is the value of x of the following after evaluation

   a. x=2
   b. x+=4
   c. x+=x+3
   d. x*=2

4. Let a, b, c be integer variables having values 12, 24, 35 respectively and x, y, z be float variables having values 10. 1, 22. 56, 32. 61 respectively. Determine the value of each arithmetic statement.

   a. a - b + c
   b. a/b%c
   c. a/b*c
   d. a % (b - c)
   e. x - y * z
   f. x % (y - z)
   g. x * y

5. Determine the value of each statement.

Let x = 21, y=52, z = 103

1. p = (y== 20)? x: z*3 2. q = (x*3 >= 0)? y-9: z+2

3.4 Input Output Functions in C

Introduction:

In C language input and output functions are accomplished through library function. The header file for I/O function is <stdio. h>. In C there are two types of I/O functions. They are console I/O and file I/O. In this chapter only console I/O functions are dealt. Console I/ o function takes I/P from keyboard and produces o/p on the screen. The console Input/Output functions are also called as Standard input/output functions.

Classification:

The console I/O function are classified as shown below.

Console I/O function: two types

1. Formatted function 2. unformatted function:

Example: scanf two types: 1) Char I/O 2) String I/O functions

Printf

1. *Character oriented i/o functions*
   Examples: getchar( ) , putchar( ), getch( ), getche( )

2. String I/O functions
   Examples: gets(), puts()

3.4.1 Formatted Input/Output Functions

Formatted I/O functions means reading and writing data in formats which are desired by the user. The function used to input action is scanf( ) and output action is printf( ).

The printf() Function

printf () is used to print or display data on the console in a formatted form. The format of printf () is

printf ("control string", list of arguments);

Control string contains the formatting instructions within quotes.

This can contain

i. Characters that are simply printed as they are
ii. Conversion specifications with begins with format specifier (%) sign.
iii. Escape sequences.

Arguments values get substituted in the place of appropriate format specifications. Arguments can be variables, constants, arrays or complex expressions. The percentage (%) followed by conversion character is called format specifier. This indicates the type of the corresponding data item.

In the table 3. 4. 1 most frequently used format specifiers are listed.

Table 3. 4. 1

Format specifier or format string or control string	*meaning*
% d or % i	decimal numbers or integers
% u	unsigned decimal integer
% x	unsigned hexadecimal value (lower case letter)
% X	unsigned hexadecimal value (upper case letter)
% o	octal number
% c	character constant

Continued...

% f	floating point number (single precision)
% s	strings
% lf	double precision floating point
% ld	long signed integer numbers
% lu	long unsigned integer numbers
% p	displays pointer
% %	displays a % sign
% e	displays scientific notation (e lower case)
% E	displays scientific notation (e upper case)

Application of printf() Function

The printf() function is used to print the different types of output. This is given below.

i. Printing given data

ii. The printf() statement can be used without format specifier, just to print the given data. This is as shown below.

```
printf (“C programming is easy”);
Output:
C programming is easy
```

iii. Printing numbers

To print integers % d or % I is used to print floating point % f is used. This is as shown below.

```
int a = 5
float d = 10. 3;
printf(“the value of integer a is %d’, a);
printf(“the value of float d is %f’, d);
```

Output:

The value of integer a is5
The value of float is 10. 3

In the above instance instead of using two printf() statements only one printf() can be used. This is as shown below

printf("the value of integer a is %d \n, the value of float d is %f" a, d);

Output:

The value of integer a is 5
The value of float is 10. 3

iv. Printing character/string data

To print character % c used and to print a string % s format specifier is used. This is shown below.

printf("this is % c %s", 'a', "book");

The characters are always given in single quote and strings are enclosed in quote (double).

Escape Sequence in printf () Function

In addition to format specification, escape sequence can also be used in printf(). These are specified in the control string portion of the printf() and are used mainly for screen formatting. All escape sequence are provided with slash (/). Since back slash is considered as an "escape" character. These sequences are called escape sequences. These sequences cause an escape from the normal interpretation of a string. So that the next character (after blank slash) is recognized as having a special meaning.

- Usage of \t moves the cursor to next tab problem
- \n makes the cursor to go to new line.

- \r moves the cursor to the beginning of the line in which it is currently placed.
- \a alters the user by sounding the inbuilt speaker of system.
- \b moves the cursor one position to the left of its current opposition.
- the character of single quote and back slash can be printed by using escape sequence \', \", \\ respectively.

i. printf ("Professor asked, \" did you understand the concept?\" ");

   This will print

   Professor asked, "did you understand the concept ?"

ii. printf (" The sequences is a>b, where \'ba\' is >10");

   This will print

   The sequence is a>b, where 'ba' is >10

iii. printf("Hello,\n How do \n You do?");

   This will print

   Hello

   How do

   You do

Minimum Field Width Specifier (MFWS)

An integer placed between the % sign and format code is called minimum field width specifier or % number format code; ex. %5d. If string or number to be printed is longer than that minimum it will printed as such. Minimum field width specifiers are used to make the O/P such that it reaches the minimum length specified. This is done by padding. Default padding is done with spaces. This is used most commonly produce table in which column line up.

If we wish to pad the space (if any) with zeros, place zero before MFWS. For example %d, will pad a number with 'zeros' if numbers is less than five digits. So that the total length is 5. %d will pad a number with 'space'. If number is less than five digits. So that the total length is five.

The following example demonstrates the working of minimum field width specifier.

Double count;

Count = 210. 61325;// here total digits are 8, includes dot (.) operators.

printf (" %f", count);

printf (" %10f", count);

printf (" %010f", count);

Output

210. 61325

210. 61325// inserts 2 blank spaces. So that total length = 10 digits

0210. 61325// inserts 2 zeros. So that total length = 10 digits

The Precision Specifier

Precision specifier follows minimum field width specifier (if given). It consists of a period followed by an integer (i. e. for ex %5. 1d). the way it works depends upon data types used. When precision is applied to float data, it determines the number of decimal places displayed. For example % 8. 5f displays a number at least 8 character width with four decimal places. When precision is applied to string, the precision specifier species maximum field length. For example %5. 9S, displays a string at least five and not exceeding of characters long. If string is longer than the maximum field width the end character are truncated, so that string length is equal to integer types. The precision specifier determines the minimum number of digits. That appears for the given number. Leading zeros are added to achieve the required number of digits.

```
printf("5. 4f\n", 716. 012354817);
printf("2. 8d\n", 5214);
printf("8. 12S\n", "This is Programming book");
```

Output

```
716. 0123543817
00005214
This is Programming book
```

The scanf() Function

The scanf() reads the input data from standard input device. i. e. keyboard. The syntax of the scanf() function is

scanf("format string" , list of arguments);

Where format string consists of format specifier and arguments consists of address of variables. To this corresponding address the data read from keyboard is sent. The address of the variable is denoted by ampersand symbol '&' (it is called as address of the operator).

Note: The values that are supplied through keyboard must be separated by either blank tabs or newlines. Escape sequences are not included in scanf() function.

i. To read integer data:

   ```
   int a ;
   scanf("%d", &a);
   ```

ii. To read floating point data:

```
float fc;
scanf("%f", &fc);
```

iii. To read character data;

```
char sams, johns;
scanf("%c", &sams, &johns);
```

iv. To read more than one data types at a time

```
int ia;
float ba;
char ca;
char sa[30];
scanf("%d %f %c %s", &ia, &ba, &ca, &sa);
```

3.4.2 Unformatted I/O Function

A simple reading of data from keyboard and writing to I/O device, without any format is called unformatted I/O functions. This is classified as string I/O and character I/O.

Character Input/Output(I/O)

In order to read and output a single character character I/O functions are used. The functions under character I/O are

i. getchar( )

ii. putchar( )

iii. getch( )

iv. getche()

The getchar( ) function

Single characters can be entered into the computer using the C library function getchar( ). The getchar( ) function is a part of the standard

C Input/Output library. It returns a single character from a standard input device typically a keyboard. The function does not require any arguments, though a pair of empty parentheses must follow the word getchar( ).

The syntax is

```
character variable=getchar( );
```

Where character variable refers to some previously declared character variable.

Example:

A C program contains the following statements

```
char ch;

ch=getchar( );
```

The first statement declares that c is a character-type variable. The second statement causes a single character to be entered from the standard input device and then assigned to c. If an end-of-file condition is encountered when reading a character with getchar function, the value of the symbolic constant EOF will automatically be returned. (This value will be assigned within the stdio. h file. Typically, EOF will be assigned the value -1, though this may vary from one compiler to another).

The getchar function can also be used to read multi character strings, by reading one character at a time within a multi pass loop.

```
int ia, ja; char aa, ba; ia = 66;
b = 'h'
ja = getchar( );
aa = getchar( );
putchar(ba);
putchar(aa);
putchar(ja);
```

Output:

```
h
b
- (based on input)
```

Drawback: getchar() is that buffers the input until 'ENTER' key is pressed. This means that **getchar** does not see the character until the user presses return. This is called line buffered input. This line buffering may leave one or more characters waiting in the input queue, which leads to 'errors' in interactive environment. Hence alternatives to getchar() is used.

The putchar( ) function

Single characters can be displayed using the C library function putchar. This function is complementary to the character input function getchar. The putchar function, like getchar, is a part of the standard C I/O library. It transmits a single character to a standard output device. The character being transmitted will normally be represented as a character type variable. It must be expressed as an argument to the function, enclosed in parentheses, following the word putchar.

The syntax is
putchar(character variable);

where character variable refers to some previously declared character variable.

A C program contains the following statements

```
Char c;
putchar(c);
```

If putchar() is called with integer value, the equivalent ASCII character is displayed.

```
Example: int ia, ja; char aa, ba; ia = 66;
b = 'h'
```

```
ja = getchar( );
aa = getchar( );
putchar(ba);
putchar(aa);
putchar(ja);
```

Alternatives to getchar( )

The two common alternative functions to getchar( ) are

1. getch( )
2. getche( )

The *getch( )* function reads a single character at a time and it waits for key press. It does not echo the character on the screen.

The getche( ) is same as getch( )/ but the key is echoed. This is illustrated below.

```
char che;
che = getch( )// let key press = k
putchar(che);
Output:
(nothing is displayed)
char che;
che = getche()// let key press = k
putchar(che);

Output:

k
```

String I/O

In order to read and write string of characters the functions gets() and puts() are used gets() function reads the string and puts() function takes the string as argument and writes on the screen. This is illustrated below

```
char names [50]
puts ("Enter your favourite cricketer name");
gets (names);
puts(" The name you entered is ")
puts(names);
```

Output:

```
Enter your name: M S Dhoni  /* string as entered by user*/
The name you entered is: M S Dhoni
```

3.5 Type Conversion in C

Type casting or Type conversion means conversion/transformation from one data type to another data type either for promotion or demotion. There are two types of type conversion:

1. Implicit Type Conversion:

It is also known as automatic type conversion.

- Done by the compiler on its own, without any external trigger from the user.
- Generally takes place when in an expression more than one data type is present. In such condition type conversion (type promotion) takes place to avoid lose of data.
- All the data types of the variables are upgraded to the data type of the variable with largest data type.
- char -> short int -> int -> unsigned int -> long -> unsigned -> long long -> float -> double -> long double
- It is possible for implicit conversions to lose information, signs can be lost (when signed is implicitly converted to unsigned), and overflow can occur (when long long is implicitly converted to float).

Example:

```
#include<stdio. h>
void main( )
{
        int ia=12;
        printf("%f", ia);
}
```

Output:

12. 000000

2. Explicit Type Conversion– This process is also called type casting and it is user defined. Here the user can type cast the result to make it of a particular data type.

The syntax in C:

(type) expression

Type indicated the data type to which the final result is converted.

```
// C program to demonstrate explicit type casting or conversion
#include<stdio. h>
int main()
{
    double x = 1. 2;
    // Explicit conversion from double to int
    int sum = (int)x + 1;
    printf("sum = %d", sum);
    return 0;
}
```

Advantages of Type Conversion:

- This is done to take advantage of certain features of type hierarchies or type representations.

CHAPTER 4

Statements

4.1 Introduction

STATEMENT:

It's an instruction that indicates a task or an operation. Every statement ends with a semicolon(;).

4.2 Types of Statements

C language supports different statements

Some are

a. Null statement
b. Expression statement
c. Return statement
d. Compound statement
e. Declaration statement
f. Conditional statement

a) Null statement:

just putting or writing a semicolon is called Null statement. It indicates nothing that's why it is also called empty statement.

Eg: ;//Null statement

b) Expression statement:

Placing semicolon after writing an expression is called expression statement. The expression can be any valid C expression.

Eg: x=y=z;

```
Variable+6;
A++ + --B;
c=a+b;
```

c) Return statement:

This statement is used to terminate the function. All the user defined functions should have a return statement at the end of the function.

Syntax:
return variable/expression/constant;
In the syntax return is a keyword.

Eg: return sum;// sum is variable. The value of sum will be returned.

return a+b-c;// The expression a+b-c is evaluated and then that value will be returned.

return 5. 78;// returns value 5. 78

d) Compound statement:

It is also called a Block. group of statements enclosed with in flower braces is called compound statement. compound statements can contain another compound statements with in it.

Eg:

```
{
        x=y=z;
                Variable+6;
                A++ + --B;
                c=a+b;
}
```

e) Declaration statement:

This statement tells about the name, data type of an identifier to the compiler before it's use in the program. During declaration memory is not reserved for an identifier, but it will be reserved during definition.

Eg: auto int a;//declaration statement
int a;// definition statement

f) conditional statement:

The statement which has condition is called conditional statement.

4.3 Conditional Statements

it's also called as ***decision making statements*** or ***selection statements***. This statement is used when we want to make a decision or to change the automatic flow of program control.

The conditional statements in C language are

i. if statement

ii. switch statement

if statement:

It's a conditional statement. The different forms of if statements are

→ simple if
→ if else
→ nested if else
→ if else if ladder
→ **simple if statement:**

Syntax:

```
if(expression)
{
        Statement1;
```

```
            ---------------
            ---------------
            statement n;
    }
```

Explanation:

The expression in the if statement should be either relational(eg: a>0 or a>b) or logical (eg: a>b && a>c) expression.

The expression is evaluated first and if it results true then the statements under if condition are executed and come out of if statement and executes the remaining statements of the program.

If the expression results false then it skips the if statement part and executes the remaining statements of the program.

We can have single or multiple statements under if condition. if we have multiple statements then these statements should be enclosed with in flower braces.

If we have only one statement the we may or may not include that statement within the flower brace.

Program:

Write a C program to find small number of two numbers.

```
#include<stdio. h>
void main()
{
        int ia, ib;
        printf("enter two numbers");
        scanf("%i%i",&ia,&ib);// use %i as format specifier for integers
        if(ia<ib)
        printf("\n %i is small value ", ia);
        if(ib<ia)
        printf("\n %d is small value ", ib);
}
```

→ if else statement:

It's another kind of if statement. it is a two way selection statement. it is an alternative to conditional operator.

Syntax:

```
if(expression)
{
            statement t1;
            --------------
            statement tn;
      }
      else
      {
            statement f1;
            --------------
            statement fn;
}
```

Explanation:

In this statement first expression will be evaluated. if the expression evaluates to true then statements under if condition are executed otherwise statements under else part will be executed.

Flow chart:

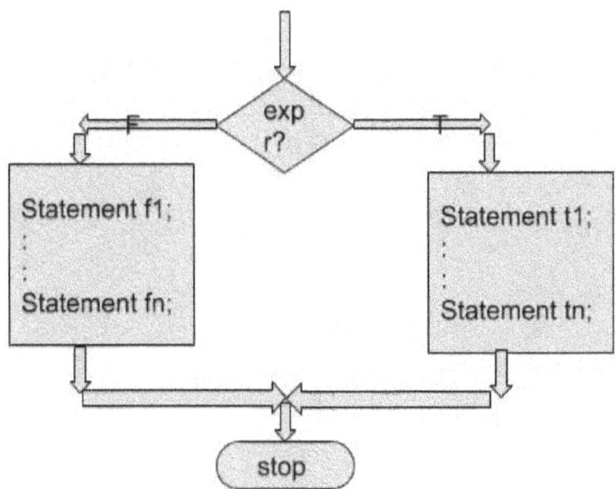

Programs:

1. Write a C program to find big number of two numbers or values using if else statement

```
#include<stdio. h>
void main()
{
        int ia, ib;
        printf("enter two numbers");
        scanf("%i%i",&ia,&ib);
        if(ia<ib)
        printf("\n %d is big value", ib);
        else
        printf("\n %d is big value", ia);
}
```

2. Write a C program to check whether the given character is vowel or not using if else statement.

```
#include<stdio. h>
void main()
{
        char ch ;
        int ans;
        printf("enter any character");
        scanf("%c",&ch);
        ans=(ch=='a'||ch=='A'||ch=='e'||ch=='E'||ch=='i'||ch=='I'||ch=='o
        '||ch=='O'||ch=='u'||ch=='U');
        if(ans==1)
        printf("\n %c is a vowel character", ch);
        else
        printf("\n %c is not a vowel character", ch);
}
```

→ nested if else statement:

An if else statement or if statement contains another if else statement with in it then such if else called nested if else statement or nested if statement. The nested if else can contain any number of if statements or if else statements either under if part or else part. This statement used when we want to specify more number conditions to provide more options. It is also called as multi way selection statement.

Syntax:

```
if(expression1)
{
        if(expression2)
        Statement1;
        else
        Statement2;
}
else
Statement3;
```

Program:

Write a C program to biggest number among three numbers.

```
#include<stdio. h>
void main()
{
        int a, b, c;
        printf("enter three numbers");
        scanf("%d%d%d",&a,&b,&c);
        if(a>b)
        {
                if(a>c)
                printf("\n %d is small number", a);
                else
                printf("\n %d is small number", c);
        }
```

```
        else
        {
                if(b>c)
                 printf("\n %d is small number", b);
                else
                printf("\n %d is small number", c);
        }
}
```

Dangling else problem:

Once if we use if else statement, we encounter a problem called dangling else problem.

This problem will arise when there is no matching else for every if statement. The solution to this problem is that always pair else to the most recent unpared if in the current block.

Eg:

```
        if(expr1)
        if(expr2)
        Statement1;
        else
        Statement2;
```

Solution:

```
if(expr1)
{
        if(expr2)
                Statement1;
        else
                Statement2;
}
```

→ if else if ladder statement:

It is also called multi way selection statement. it is an alternative to nested if statement.

Syntax:

```
if(expr1)
Statementblock1;
        else if (expr2)
                Statementblock2;
                :
                :
                :
                else
                        Statementblockn;
```

Explanation:

In this the expressions are executed from first to last. whenever the expression evaluates true then the corresponding statement block will be executed and come out of the if else if ladder process. if that expression is false we move to next expression and evaluate it. if all the expressions evaluate false then last else part will be executed. The statement may have single or multiple statements.

Flow chart:

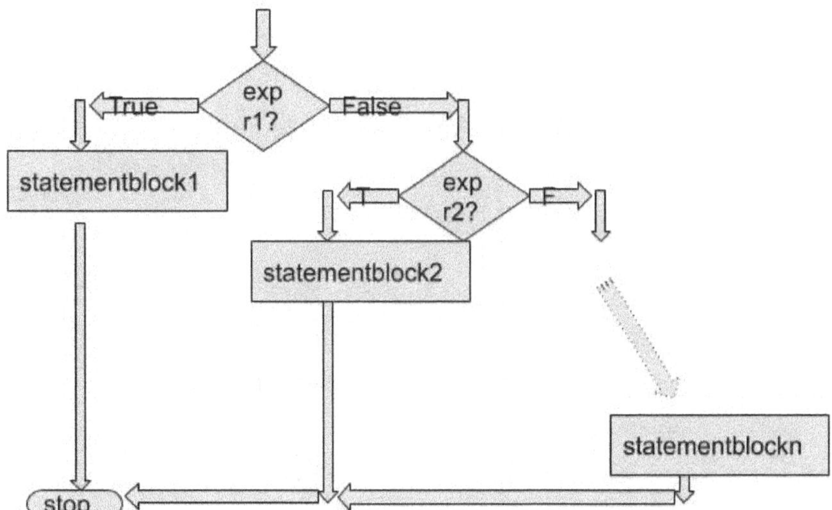

Programs:

1. Write a C program to accept five subject marks and then calculate the total, average. Display the total marks, average marks and result based on the following criteria.

Average	Result
>=70	distinction
60-70	first class
50-60	second class
40-50	third class

```
#include<stdio. h>
void main()
{
        int a, b, c, d, e, total;
        float avg;
        printf("enter five subject marks");
        scanf("%d%d%d%d%d",&a,&b,&c,&d,&e);
        if(a<35||b<35||c<35||d<35||e<35)
        printf("\n fail");
        else
        {
                total=a+b+c+d+e;
                avg=(float)total/5;//type conversion
                if(avg>=70)
                        printf("\n distinction");
                else if(avg>=60)
                        printf("\n first class");
                else if(avg>=50)
                        printf("\n second class");
                else
                        printf("\n third class");
        }
}
```

2. Write a C program to find the roots of a quadratic equation.

```
#include<stdio. h>
#include<math. h>
void main()
{
        int a, b, c, d;
        float r1, r2;
        printf("enter a, b, c values");
        scanf("%d%d%d",&a,&b,&c);
        d=b*b-4*a*c;
        if(d==0)
        {
        printf("\n roots are real and equal");
        r1=-b/(2*a);
        r2=r1;
        printf("\n root1 value=%f, root2 value=%f", r1, r2);
        }
        else if(d>0)
        {
        printf("\n roots are real and unequal");
        r1=(-b+sqrt(d))/(2*a);
        r2=(-b-sqrt(d))/(2*a);
        printf("\n root1 value=%f, root2 value=%f", r1, r2);
        }
        else
        {
        printf("\n roots are imaginary");
        r1=-b/(2*a);
        r2=sqrt(abs(d))/(2*a);
        printf("\n root1 value=%f+i%f, root2 value=%f-i%f", r1, r2, r1,
        r2);
        }
}
```

Exercise:

1. Write a C program to display the day of a week based on number.

2. Write a C program to generate electricity bill amount based on the following constraints

Consumed Units	amount
<100	Rs. 1. 60/unit
100-200	Rs. 2. 35/unit
201-400	Rs. 3. 40/unit
>400	Rs. 5. 25/unit

→ Switch statement:

It is another conditional statement and multiway branching statement. This statement is used when there is a possibility to make a choice from several alternatives. This statement accepts only one integral expression. integral expression always gives an integer value as a result. The expression can have a single variable.

Syntax:

```
switch(expression)
{
case constant1: statementblock1;break;
case constant2: statementblock2;break;
:                :      :              :
:                :      :              :
case constantn: statementblockn;break;
        default: statementx;
}
```

In switch statement,

- First the switch expression will be evaluated and that valued will be compared with all the case constants for equality in a sequence.

if any case constant matches with expression value then the corresponding statement block gets executed and come out of the switch statement process otherwise go for next match.

- If none of the case constants match with expression value then default statement block gets executed.
- Case indicates an option or choice. constant must be integer or character.
- The default statement can be written anywhere in the switch statement.
- Break statement causes an exit from switch statement. if break statement not present in the switch then all the statements are executed in sequence with checking case constants.
- No need enclose flower braces for multiple statements in statement blocks.

Programs:

1. Write a C program to check whether the given number is even or not using switch statement.

```
#include<stdio. h>
void main()
{
        int n, r;
        printf(" enter a number");
        scanf("%d",&n);
        r=n%2;
        switch(r)
        {
        case 0: printf("\n %i is an even value ", n);break;
        default: printf("\n %i is not an even value ", n);break;
        }
}
```

2. Write a C program to check whether the given character is vowel or not using switch statement.

```
#include<stdio. h>
void main()
{
        char ch;
        printf(" enter a number");
        scanf("%c",&ch);
        switch(ch)
        {
            case 'a':
            case 'A':
            case 'e':
            case 'E':
            case 'i':
            case 'I':
            case 'o':
            case 'O':
            case 'u':
            case 'U': printf("\n %c is a vowel", ch);break;
            default: printf("\n %d is not a vowel", ch);break;
        }
}
```

Exercise:

1. Write a C program to the day names of a week based on a number.
2. Write a C program to the month names of a year based on a number.
3. Write a C program to input two numbers and an arithmetic operator based on operator, corresponding arithmetic

operation should be performed and that result should be displayed using switch statement.

4. Write a C program to display the rainbow colors based on character.

5. Write a C program to input a two digit number and display it in words(for eg, input is 10 it should display ten).

4.4 Looping Statements

These statements are also called iterative statements or repetitive statements.

Looping means executing a statement or set of statements repeatedly until a specified condition becomes false.

Generally the loop control statements has two things. one thing is body of the loop which to be executed repeatedly and second thing is the condition which is tested for termination of the loop.

Loop control statements are two types

- Pretest loop
- Post test loop

Pretest loop:

In this first we test the condition. If it is true then the body of the loop gets executed and then we test the condition again. This process will be repeated until the specified condition becomes false. when the condition becomes false, we come out of the looping process.

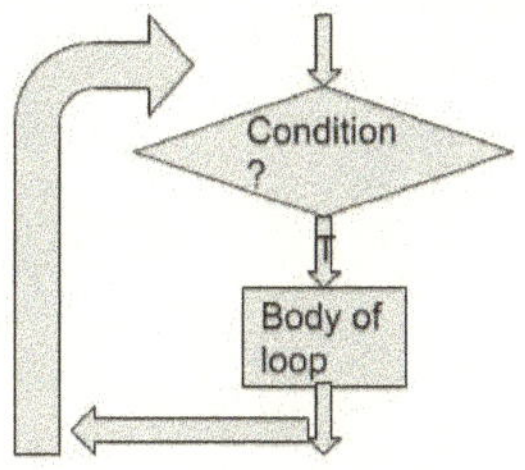

Posttest loop:

In this the body of the loop executed first, later we check the condition. if the condition is true then the body of the loop executed. This process will be repeated until the specified condition becomes false. when the condition becomes false, we come out of the looping process.

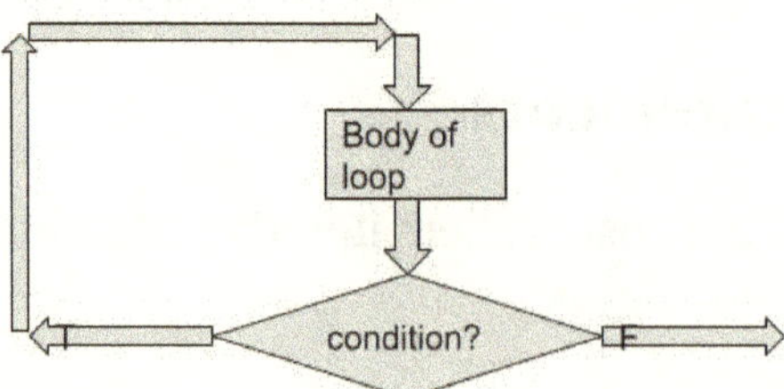

In C language, Every loop control statement contains three things

- Loop variable initialization: loop variable has to be initialized with initial value or final value.

  Eg: i=5;
  j=i+1;

- Loop condition: it can be a relational expression or logical expression

  Eg: i>0
  i>10 &&j<100

- Loop variable increment/decrement operation(Updation Statement): In this we can increment or decrement the value of variable using increment/decrement operators.

  Eg: i++;
  J--;

4.4.1 While Loop

It's a pretest loop or entry control loop.

Syntax:

```
Initialization;
While (condition)
{
        Statement1;
        Statement2;
        --------------
        UpdationStatement;
}
```

In the while loop, first the initialization statement gets executed, then condition is verified if that is true then statement1, statement2 .... updation statement. all the statements (body of while loop) gets executed. After that again the condition will be verified if it's false then we stop the process otherwise the execution continues.

Flow Chart:

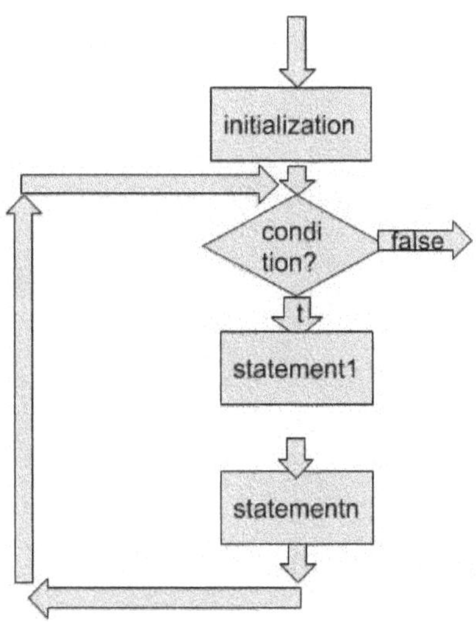

Programs:

1. Write a C program to print first n natural numbers.

```
#include<stdio. h>
void main()
{
        int n, i;
        printf("enter n value");
        scanf("%d",&n);
        printf("\n first %d natural numbers are:");
        i=1;
        while(i<=n)
        {
        printf("%d\t", i);// \t is for tab space between the numbers
        i++;
        }
}
```

2. Write a C program to find sum of n natural numbers.

```
#include<stdio. h>
void main()
{
        int n, i, sum=0;
        printf("enter n value");
        scanf("%d",&n);
        i=1;
        while(i<=n)
        {
        sum=sum+i++;
        }
printf("\n sum of %d natural numbers value=%d", sum);
}
```

3. Write a C program to find the factorial of a given number

```
#include<stdio. h>
void main()
{
        int n, i;
long int f;
        printf("enter n value");
        scanf("%d",&n);
                f=1;
        while(i<=n)
        {
        f*=i;
        i++;
        }
printf("\n factorial of %d value=%ld", n. f);
}
```

4. Write a C program to find the sum of the digits of a given number.

```
#include<stdio. h>
void main()
{
        int n, i, d, sum=0, t;
        printf("enter n value");
        scanf("%d",&n);
        t=n;
        while(n>0)
        {
             d=n%10;// find the digit
             sum+=d;
             n/=10;// update the number
        }
printf("\n sum of digits of %d value=%d", t, sum);
}
```

5. Write a C program to find the reverse number of a given number

```
#include<stdio. h>
void main()
{
        int n, i, d, sum=0, t;
        printf("enter n value");
        scanf("%d",&n);
        t=n;
        while(n>0)
        {
            d=n%10;// find the digit
            sum=sum*10+d;
            n/=10;// update the number
        }
printf("\n The reverse number of a given number %d is %d", t, sum);
}
```

Exercise:

1. Write a C program to check whether the given number is prime number or not.
2. Write a C program to check whether the given number is strong number or not.
3. Write a C program to check whether the given number is palindrome number or not.
4. Write a C program to check whether the given number is perfect number or not.
5. Write a C program to check whether the given number is Armstrong number or not.

4.4.2 Do While Loop

It's a post test loop and exit control loop.

Syntax:

```
Initialization;
do
{
        Statement1;
        :
        :
        Upadationstatement;
} while(condition);
```

In this like while loop the initialization statement gets executed later all the statements of do while(body of do while loop) loop get executed and then loop condition is tested if it's true then the body of do while loop gets executed otherwise the looping process stops.

FlowChart:

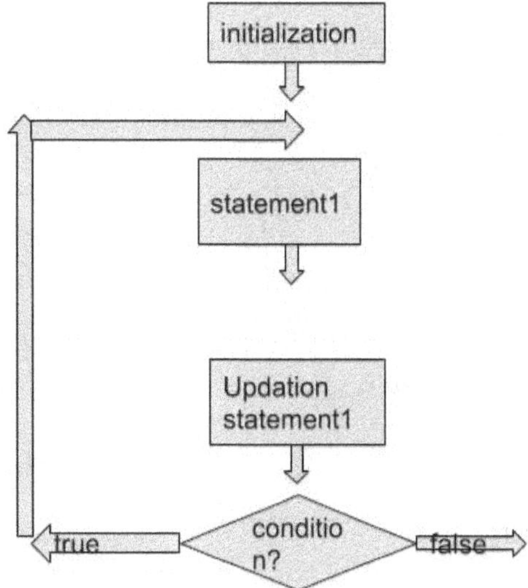

Program:

1. Write a C program to display numbers from 1 to 10 using do while statement

```
#include<stdio. h>
void main()
{
        int n, i;
        printf("enter n value");
        scanf("%d",&n);
        printf("\n first 10 natural numbers are:");
        i=1;
        do
        {
                printf("%d\t", i);// \t is for tab space between the numbers
                i++;
        }while(i<=10);
}
```

Exercise:

1. State the differences between while and do while loops.
2. Write a C program to print n terms of fibonacci series.

4.4.3 For Loop

It is a pretest loop and entry control loop.

Syntax:

```
for(initialization;condition;updation)
{
        Statement1;
        Statement2;
        :
        Statementn;
}
```

In the **for loop**, first initialization part will be executed, next condition is checked if it is true then all the statements in the body of the loop executed in a sequence, after that updation gets executed and again condition is verified if it is true then the body of the loop executed otherwise the looping process stops.

Flowchart:

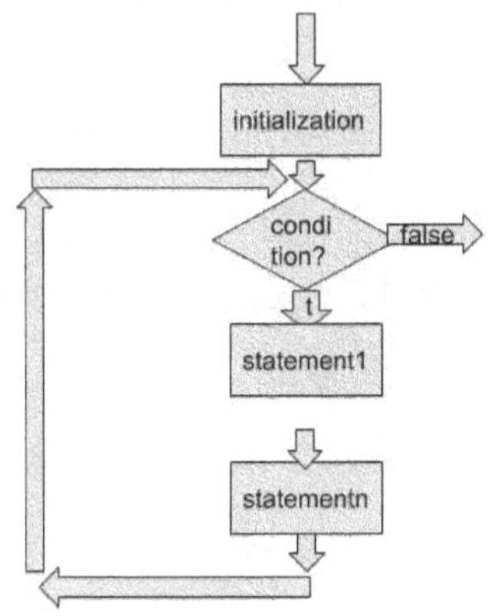

Programs:

1. Write a C program to print numbers from 35 to 12 using for loop.

```
#include<stdio. h>
void main()
{
        int i;
        for(i=35;i>=12;i--)
        printf("%d\t", i);
}
```

2. Write a C program to print multiplication table of a given number upto n terms

```
#include<stdio. h>
void main()
{
        int n, i;
```

```
        printf("enter n value");
        scanf("%d",&n);
        printf("\n multiplication table of %d is:", n);
        printf("\-----------------------------------------");
        for(i=1;i<=10;i++)
        {
                printf("\n %d * %d=%d", n, i, n*i);
        }
        printf("\-----------------------------------------");
}
```

3. Write a C program to find factorial of a given number using for loop.

```
#include<stdio. h>
void main()
{
        int n, i;
        long int f=1;
        printf("enter n value");
        scanf("%d",&n);
        for(i=1;i<=n;i++)
        f*=i;
        printf("\n factorial of %d is %ld", n, f);
}
```

Note: Placing of flower braces are optional when body of any loop statement contains only one statement.

4. Write a C program to print n terms of a fibonacci series using for loop

(fibonacci series is 0, 1, 1, 2, 3, 5, 8, 13, 21, 34, 55,..........)

```
#include<stdio. h>
void main()
{
        int n, i, a, b, c;
```

```
        printf("enter upto what terms you want to print the fibonacci
        series");
        scanf("%d",&n);
        a=0, b=1;
        printf("\n first %d terms of fibonacci series is:");
        if(n==1)
        printf("0");
        else if(n==2)
        printf("1");
        else
        {
                printf("\n 0\t 1\t");
                for(i=3;i<=n;i++)
                {
                        c=a+b;
                        printf("%d\t", c);
                        a=b;
                        b=c;
                }
        }
}
```

5. Write a C program to find the sum of the following series

1+x^2/2!+x^4/4!+x^6/6!+..........................

```
#include<stdio. h>
void main()
{
        int n, i, x;
        float term, sum;
        printf("enter number of terms(n), x value");
        scanf("%d%d",&n,&x);
        term=1. 0, sum=0. 0;
        for(i=1;i<=n;i++)
```

```
        {
        sum+=term;
        term=(term*x*x)/(2*i*(2*i-1));
        }
printf("\n sum of the given series is %f", sum);
}
```

Exercise:

1. Write a C program to find the following series
   1+2+3+4+-------------------
2. Write a C program to find the following series
   1-2+3-4+5-6+-----------------------
3. Write a C program to find the following series
   1^1+2^2+3^3+4^4+...

Note:

For loop variations:

1. for(i=1;i<=n;i++)

```
        {

        }
```

Is similar to

for(i=1;i<=n;i++);

This for loop has no body

2. Infinite loop:

The loop executed infinite number of times

Ex: for(;;)

```
{
        Statements;
}
```

3. Missing Initialization or updation statements also valid

Ex1: i=1;

```
for(;i<=n;i++)
{
        Statements;
}
```

Ex2:

```
for(i=1;i<=n;)
{
        Statements;
        i++;
}
```

4. Multiple initializations, updations are valid.

```
Ex: for(i=1, j=5, k=9;i<=9;i++, j--, k++)
{
        Statements;
}
```

5. Multiple conditions can be combined using logical operators.

Ex1: valid

```
for(i=1;i>0&&i<=9;i++)
{
        statements;
}
```

Ex2: Invalid

```
for(i=1;i>0, I<=9;i++)
{
        Statements;
}
```

4.4.4 Nested Loops

If any loop statement contains any other loop or same loop in any number of times then it is called Nested loop concept.

Ex1:

```
initialization1;
while(condition1)
{
------
initialization2;
while(condition2)
{
        ----------
        Statements;
        updation;
}
Statements;
Updation;
}
```

Ex2:

```
for(initialization1;condition1;Updation1)
{
------
initialization2;
while(condition2)
{
        ----------
        Statements;
        updation2;
}
Statements;
}
```

Programs:

1. Write a C program to print the following pattern using nested loops concept

```
****

****

****

****
```

```
#include<stdio. h>
void main()
{
        int i, j;
        for(i=1;i<=4;i++)//outer loop for rows
        {
                printf("\n");
                for(j=1;j<=4;j++)//inner loop for columns
                printf("*");
        }
}
```

2. Write a C program to print the following pattern using nested loops concept

```
1
12
123
1234
12345
```

```
#include<stdio. h>
void main()
{
        int i, j;
```

```
        for(i=1;i<=5;i++)//outer loop for rows
        {
        printf("\n");
        for(j=1;j<=i;j++)//inner loop for columns
        printf("%d", i);
        }
}
```

3. Write a C program to print the following FLOYD'S Triangle.

```
1
23
456
78910
#include<stdio. h>
void main()
{
        int i, j, k=1;
        for(i=1;i<=4;i++)//outer loop for rows
        {
                printf("\n");
                for(j=1;j<=i;j++)//inner loop for columns
                printf("%d", k++);
        }
}
```

4. Write a C program to print all the prime numbers from 1 to n

```
#include<stdio. h>
void main()
{
        int i, j, n, count;
        printf("enter n value");
        scanf("%d",&n);
        for(i=1;i<=n;i++)//outer loop for rows
        {
```

```
            count=0;
            for(j=1;j<=i;j++)//inner loop for columns
            {
                  if(i%j==0)
                  count++;
            }
      if(count==2)
      printf(\n%d", i);
      }
}
```

Exercise:

1. Write a C program to display the following pattern

54321
4321
321
21
1

2. Write a C program to display the following pattern

1
22
333
4444
55555
666666

3. Write a C program to display the following pattern

5
54
543
5432
54321

4. Write a C program to display the following pattern

```
54321
 5432
  543
   54
    5
```

5. Write a C program to display the following Pascal's Triangle pattern

```
         1
      1     1
   1     2     1
1     3     3     1
```

4.5 Jump Statements

These statements are also called unconditional statements. These statements are used to transfer the program control from one position to another.

Jump statements are

- break
- continue
- goto

break statement: break is a keyword used in the loops and switch statement to terminate or coming out of the process.

Syntax: break;

Ex:
```
for(i=1;i<=5;i++)
    {
        if(i==3)
        break;
        printf("%d\t", i);

    }
```

output: 1   2

continue statement: This statement does not terminate the process but only skips current iteration round of the loop.

Syntax: continue;

```
Ex: for(i=1;i<=5;i++)
        {
                if(i==3)
                continue;
                printf("%d\t", i);
        }
```

output: 1 2 4 5

goto statement:

This statement is used to transfer the program control from one position to another.

These are two types

- Forward goto or forward jump
- Backward goto or Backward jump

Forward goto Syntax:

```
goto labelname;

        ---------
        ---------
        ---------

labelname:

        ----------
        ---------
        ---------
```

Backward goto Syntax:

```
labelname:

        ----------
        ---------
        ---------

goto labelname;

        ---------
        ---------
        ---------
```

Note: labelname is a valid identifier

```
Ex: #include<stdio. h>
void main()
{
        int age;
        Y:
                printf("enter your age");
                scanf("%d",&age);
                if(age>=18)
                goto X;
                else
                printf("\n you are not eligible for vote");
                goto Y;
        X:
printf("\n you are eligible for vote");
}
```

CHAPTER 5

Arrays

5.1 Introduction

Array: It is a derived datatype. It is nothing but collection of homogeneous elements under a single name. It is a finite set of values of same data type.

Types of Arrays

1. One dimensional arrays(1D arrays)
2. Two dimensional arrays(2D arrays)
3. Multi dimensional arrays

5.2 One Dimensional Arrays

Properties:

- **Declaration of 1d array:**
  Syntax: datatype arrayname[array_size];
  Ex: int A[10];
  float B[20];
  char C[5];
- Every array is uniquely identified by a name. every name is an identifier. In the above example A, B, C are array names.
- Array_size means the number of elements that array can hold or it indicates the capacity of the array
  In the above example 10, 20, 5 indicates array_size

- The individual elements of an array are identified by index or subscript. Index or subscript is an integer value.
- Every array index begins with zero(0).
- Syntax: arrayname[index];
  Ex: A[0] denotes first element of the array, similarly A[3] denotes fourth element of the array.
- Array A

5	3	6	4
A[0]	A[1]	A[2]	A[3]

- All the array elements are stored in contiguous memory locations(no gap in memory addresses)
- Ex:

5	3	6	4
Address 100	102	104	106

- The starting address of the array is called ***base address*** of the array.
- Ex: from the above example base address is 100
  We can get it by writing &A[0] or A
- The memory required or occupied by an array is calculated as array_size × size of (array datatype)
  Ex: int A[10];
  Memory required by an array A = 10 × size of (int)
  = 20
- The address of individual elements of the array is calculated as Address of A[index]=baseaddress+index × size of (array datatype)
  Ex: address of A[2]=100+2 × size of (int))
  = 100+4
  = 104
- If an array contains only one index or subscript such array is called one dimensional arrays.
  Ex: A[1], b[10], C[4]

Storing values into one dimensional arrays:

We can store values into 1D arrays in 3 ways

- Assigning the values
- Initialization of an array
- Inputting the values

Assigning the values:

- We can assign the values to an array using assignment operator(=).

  Ex: A[0]=10;

  A[1]=20;

  A[2]=5;

  A[3]=40;

  Then the array A looks like this

10	20	5	40
A[0]	A[1]	A[2]	A[3]

We can't copy the entire array elements into another array directly but can be copied individually.

Ex: int A[4]={10, 20, 30, 40}, b[4];

Then b[0]=A[0];B[1]=A[1];B[2]=A[2];B[3]=A[3];

Then the array A looks like this

10	20	30	40
B[0]	B[1]	B[2]	B[3]

Initialization of an array or Array initialization:

Storing the values into an array at the declaration of the array itself is called array initialization.

Syntax: datatype arrayname[array_size]={value1, value2,......};

Ex:

1. int A[4]={10, 20, 30, 40};

10	20	30	40
A[0]	A[1]	A[2]	A[3]

2. int A[4];

Garbage value	Garbage value	Garbage value	Garbage value
A[0]	A[1]	A[2]	A[3]

3. int A[4]={10, 20};

10	20	0	0
A[0]	A[1]	A[2]	A[3]

4. int A[4]={0};

0	0	0	0
A[0]	A[1]	A[2]	A[3]

5. int A[4]={10, 20, 30, 40, 50};// you may not get the error.

6. int A[]={10, 20, 30, 40};// it is also valid

10	20	30	40
A[0]	A[1]	A[2]	A[3]

Inputting and outputting the values of1D array:

Input the values:

By using scanf() function, we can store or input the values into an array.

Ex1: int a[10];

To store 10 integer values into 1D array, we can write like this

```
for(i=0;i<10;i++)//here i denotes index value
scanf("%d",&a[i]);
```

Ex2: To store n integer values into 1D array(n must be less than size of the array), we can write like this

```
for(i=0;i<n;i++)//here i denotes index value
scanf("%d",&a[i]);
```

Output the values:

By using printf() function, we can store or input the values into an array.

Ex1: int a[10];

To display 10 integer values into 1D array, we can write like this

```
for(i=0;i<10;i++)//here i denotes index value
printf("%d", a[i]);
```

Ex2: To display n integer values into 1D array, we can write like this

```
for(i=0;i<n;i++)//here i denotes index value
printf("%d", a[i]);
```

Programs:

1. Write a C program to read and display n values of an array

```
#include<stdio. h>
void main()
{
        int a[20], i, n;
        printf("enter n value");
        scanf("%d",&n);
        printf("\n enter %d values into an array", n);
```

```
        for(i=0;i<n;i++)
        scanf("%d",&a[i]);
        printf("\n the array values are");
        for(i=0;i<n;i++)
        printf("%d\t", a[i]);
}
```

2. Write a C program to find sum, average values of an array.

```
#include<stdio. h>
Void main()
{
        int a[20], i, n, sum=0;
        float avg;
        printf("enter n value");
        scanf("%d",&n);
        printf("\n enter %d values into an array", n);
        for(i=0;i<n;i++)
        scanf("%d",&a[i]);
        printf("\n the array values are");
        for(i=0;i<n;i++)
        printf("%d\t", a[i]);
        for(i=0;i<n;i++)
        sum+=a[i];
avg=(float)sum/n;
printf("\n sum of array values=%d \n average of array values=%f",
sum, avg);
}
```

3. Write a C Program to find biggest number, smallest number of the array.

```
#include<stdio. h>
Void main()
{
        int a[20], i, n, big, small;
```

```
        printf("enter n value");
        scanf("%d",&n);
        printf("\n enter %d values into an array", n);
        for(i=0;i<n;i++)
        scanf("%d",&a[i]);
        printf("\n the array values are");
        for(i=0;i<n;i++)
        printf("%d\t", a[i]);
        big=small=a[0];
        for(i=0;i<n;i++)
        {
                if(big<a[i])
                big=a[i];
                if(small>a[i])
                small=a[i];
        }
printf("\n biggest number=%d \t smallest number=%d", big, small);
}
```

Exercise:

1. Write a C program to print alternate values of an array.
2. Write a C program to print multiples of 3 in the array
3. Write a C program to find pair of adjacent elements with difference 4 in their values.
4. Write a C program to find sum of even, odd numbers of an array.

5.3 Applications of an Array

One dimensional arrays can be used in searching and sorting methods or Techniques.

Searching:

It is a method or process to check whether the particular element is present in the array or not. The searching element is called key.

Searching methods are

- Linear search
- Binary search
- Fibonacci search

Linear Search:

It is also called Sequential search. In this the key element is compared with every element of the array one by one in a sequence till key is found or array is completed. If key is matching with array value then we say key is found, search is successful otherwise we say key is not found, search is unsuccessful.

Ex1: key=30

10	20	30	40
Key ≠ A[0]	key ≠ A[1]		key==A[2]

Key (40) is found in the array at index 2. This is successful search.

Ex2: key=3

10	20	30	40
Key ≠ A[0]	key ≠ A[1]	key ≠ A[2]	key ≠ A[3]

Key (3) is not found in the array. This is unsuccessful search.

Program:

Write a C program to implement linear search mechanism.

```
#include<stdio. h>
Void main()
{
        int a[20], i, n, key;
```

```
        printf("enter n value");
        scanf("%d",&n);
        printf("\n enter %d values into an array", n);
        for(i=0;i<n;i++)
        scanf("%d",&a[i]);
        printf("\n the array values are");
        for(i=0;i<n;i++)
        printf("%d\t", a[i]);
        printf("\n enter the key value");
        scanf('%d",&key);
        for(i=0;i<n;i++)
        {
                if(key==a[i])
                Break;
        }
        if(i==n)
        printf("\n key %d is not found in the array", key);
        else
        printf("\n key %d is found in the array", key);
}
```

Exercise:

1. Write a C program to check whether the value 3. 7 is present in the array of values or not using linear search method.
2. Write a C program to check whether the character m is present in the array of character values or not using linear search method.

Sorting:

Arranging the set of values in ascending, descending, alphabetical or dictionary order is called sorting.

Sorting Techniques are

- Bubble sort
- Selection sort
- Merge sort
- Quick sort
- Insertion sort
- Shell sort
- Radix sort

Bubble sort:

Procedure:

1. Identify the number of values in the the array(n).
2. Bubble sort has n-1 number of passes or rounds.
3. In each pass, we compare adjacent pair of elements, if they are not in our required order then we swap otherwise not. This process will continued for all the adjacent pairs in all passes.

Ex: Sort the following values in ascending order using bubble sort

3, 2, 1

3	2	1
A[0]	A[1]	A[2]

1. Array has 3(n) values, so bubble sort has 2(n-1) number of passes.

2. In pass1, first pair A[0], A[1] of elements or values compared, they are not in ascending order, so we swap.

2	3	1
A[0]	A[1]	A[2]

Now second pair of elements A[1],[2] compared, they are not in ascending order, so we swap.

2	1	3
A[0]	A[1]	A[2]

3. In pass2, first pair A[0], A[1] of elements or values compared, they are not in ascending order, so we swap.

1	2	3
A[0]	A[1]	A[2]

Now second pair of elements A[1],[2] compared, they are in ascending order already, so we don’t swap.

1	2	3
A[0]	A[1]	A[2]

After completion of two passes, the array elements are

1	2	3
A[0]	A[1]	A[2]

Program:

1. Write a C program to sort the array elements in ascending order using bubble sort technique.

```
#include<stdio. h>
Void main()
{
        int a[20], i, n, t;
        printf(“enter n value”);
        scanf(“%d”,&n);
        printf(“\n enter %d values into an array”, n);
        for(i=0;i<n;i++)
        scanf(“%d”,&a[i]);
        printf(“\n before sorting, the array values are”);
```

```
        for(i=0;i<n;i++)
        printf("%d\t", a[i]);
        for(i=1;i<n;i++)// number of passes
        {
                for(j=0;j<n;j++)// comparing adjacent pair of elements
        {
        if(a[j]>a[j+1])
                {
                        // swap a[j], a[j+1] values
                        t=a[j];
                        a[j]=a[j+1];
                        a[j+1]=t;
                }
        }
        }
        printf("\n after sorting, the array values are");
        for(i=0;i<n;i++)
        printf("%d\t", a[i]);
}
```

Exercise:

1. Write a C program to sort the array of integer elements in descending order using bubble sort.

2. Write a C program to sort the array of float elements in descending order using bubble sort.

3. Write a C program to sort the array of float elements in ascending order using bubble sort.

4. Write a C program to sort the array of character elements in alphabetical order using bubble sort.

5.4 Two Dimensional Arrays (2D arrays)

If the array contains two index values then it is called two dimensional arrays. The first index denotes row size, second index denotes column size. Generally 2D arrays are used to represent matrix or tables.

Syntax: Datatype arrayname[row_size][column_size];

Ex: int a[2][3];// it denotes matrix a of order 2×3 means a contains 2 rows and 3 columns.

- Like 1D array, 2D arrays also row, column starting index value is zero.
- The positions of 2D array a is

a0, 0	a0, 1	a0, 2
a1, 0	a1, 1	a1, 2

- a0, 0 indicates 0th row and oth column element i. e first element of the array.
- ai, j indicates ith row, jth column element.
- Memory Representation of the 2D array
- Ex: int a[2][3];

a0, 0	a0, 1	a0, 2	a1, 0	a1, 1	a1, 2
100	102	104	106	108	110

- All the 2D array elements are stored in contiguous memory locations. In the above figure 100, 102, 104, 106.... denotes the memory addresses.

Storing values into Two dimensional arrays:

We can store values into 2D arrays in 3 ways

- Assigning the values
- Initialization of an array
- Inputting the values

Assigning the values:

- We can assign the values to an array using assignment operator(=).

  Ex: A[0][0]=10;

  A[0][1]=20;

  A[0][2]=5;

  A[0][3]=40;

  Then the array A looks like this

10	20	5	40
A[0][0]	A[0][1]	A[0][2]	A[0][3]

- We can't copy the entire array elements into another array directly but can be copied individually.

  Ex: int A[1][4]={10, 20, 30, 40}, b[1][4];

  Then b[0][0]=A[0][0];B[0][1]=A[0][1];B[0][2]=A[0][2]; B[0][3] =A[0][3];

  Then the array A looks like this

10	20	30	40
B[0][0]	B[0][1]	B[0][2]	B[0][3]

Initialization of an array or Array initialization:

Storing the values into an array at the declaration of the array itself is called array initialization.

Syntax: datatype arrayname[row_size][column_size]={value1, value2,......};

Ex:

1. int A[1][4]={10, 20, 30, 40};

10	20	30	40
A[0][0]	A[0][1]	A[0][2]	A[0][3]

2. int A[1][4];

Garbage value	Garbage value	Garbage value	Garbage value
A[0][0]	A[0][1]	A[0][2]	A[0][3]

3. int A[1][4]={10, 20};

10	20	0	0
A[0][0]	A[0][1]	A[0][2]	A[0][3]

4. int A[1][4]={0};

0	0	0	0
A[0][0]	A[0][1]	A[0][2]	A[0][3]

5. int A[1][4]={10, 20, 30, 40, 50};// you may not get the error.
6. int A[][4]={10, 20, 30, 40};// it is also valid, writing of **row_size is optional**

10	20	30	40
A[0][0]	A[0][1]	A[0][2]	A[0][3]

Inputting and outputting the values of 2D array:

Input the values:

By using scanf() function, we can store or input the values into an array.

Ex1: int a[10][10];

To store 10 integer values into 2D array, we can write like this

```
for(i=0;i<10;i++)//here i denotes row index value
{
        for(j=0;j<10;j++)//here j denotes column index value
        scanf("%d",&a[i][j]);
}
```

Ex2: To store m×n integer values into 2D array(m, n must be less than row_size, cloumn_size of the 2D array), we can write like this

```
for(i=0;i<m;i++)//here i denotes row index value
{
        for(j=0;j<n;j++)//here j denotes column index value
        scanf("%d",&a[i][j]);
}
```

Output the values:

By using printf() function, we can display or print the values into an array.

To display 100 integer values into 2D array, we can write like this

```
for(i=0;i<10;i++)//here i denotes row index value
{ printf("\n");
for(j=0;j<10;j++)//here j denotes column index value
printf("%d", a[i][j]);
}
```

Ex2: To display m×n integer values into 2D array(m, n must be less than row_size, cloumn_size of the 2D array), we can write like this

```
for(i=0;i<m;i++)//here i denotes row index value
{ printf("\n");
for(j=0;j<n;j++)//here j denotes column index value
printf("%d", a[i][j]);
}
```

Programs:

1. Write a C program to read and display m×n values of matrix.

```
#include<stdio. h>
void main()
{
        int a[10][10], m, n, i, j;
        printf(" enter order of a matrix");
        scanf("%d%d",&m,&n);
        printf("\n enter values in to matrix");
        for(i=0;i<m;i++)
        {
                for(j=0;j<n;j++)
                scanf("%d",&a[i][j]);
        }
        printf("\n The matrix values are");
        for(i=0;i<m;i++)
        {
                printf("\n");
                for(j=0;j<n;j++)
                printf("%d", a[i][j]);
        }
}
```

2. Write a C program to find the transpose matrix of a given matrix of order m×n

```
#include<stdio. h>
void main()
{
        int a[10][10], m, n, i, j;
        printf(" enter order of a matrix");
        scanf("%d%d",&m,&n);
        printf("\n enter values in to matrix");
        for(i=0;i<m;i++)
```

```
        {
                for(j=0;j<n;j++)
                scanf("%d",&a[i][j]);
        }
        printf("\n The matrix values are");
        for(i=0;i<m;i++)
        {
                printf("\n");
                for(j=0;j<n;j++)
                printf("%d", a[i][j]);
        }
        printf("\n The Transpose matrix values are");
        for(i=0;i<n;i++)
        {
                printf("\n");
                for(j=0;j<m;j++)
                printf("%d", a[j][i]);
        }
}
```

3. Given two matrices of order m×nand p×q respectively. Write a C program to find addition of two matrices if possible otherwise display not possible.

```
#include<stdio. h>
void main()
{
        int a[10][10], m, n, i, j, b[10][10], p, q;
        printf(" enter order of first matrix");
        scanf("%d%d",&m,&n);
        printf("\n enter values in to first matrix");
        for(i=0;i<m;i++)
        {
        for(j=0;j<n;j++)
        scanf("%d",&a[i][j]);
```

```
}
printf("\n The first matrix values are");
for(i=0;i<m;i++)
{
        printf("\n");
        for(j=0;j<n;j++)
        printf("%d", a[i][j]);
}
printf(" enter order of second matrix");
scanf("%d%d",&p,&q);
printf("\n enter values in to second matrix");
for(i=0;i<p;i++)
{
        for(j=0;j<q;j++)
        scanf("%d",&b[i][j]);
}
printf("\n The second matrix values are");
for(i=0;i<p;i++)
{
        printf("\n");
        for(j=0;j<q;j++)
        printf("%d", b[i][j]);
}
if(m==p&&n==q)
{
        printf("\n addition of two matrices is possible");
        printf("\n The resultant matrix values are");
        for(i=0;i<p;i++)
        {
                printf("\n");
                for(j=0;j<q;j++)
                printf("%d", a[i][j]+b[i][j]);
        }
}
```

```
        else
        printf("\n addition of two matrices is not possible");
}
```

4. Given two matrices of order m×nand p×q respectively. Write a C program to find subtraction of two matrices if possible otherwise display not possible.

```
#include<stdio. h>
void main()
{
        int a[10][10], m, n, i, j, b[10][10], p, q;
        printf(" enter order of first matrix");
        scanf("%d%d",&m,&n);
        printf("\n enter values in to first matrix");
        for(i=0;i<m;i++)
        {
                for(j=0;j<n;j++)
                scanf("%d",&a[i][j]);
        }
        printf("\n The first matrix values are");
        for(i=0;i<m;i++)
        {
                printf("\n");
                for(j=0;j<n;j++)
                printf("%d", a[i][j]);
        }
        printf(" enter order of second matrix");
        scanf("%d%d",&p,&q);
        printf("\n enter values in to second matrix");
        for(i=0;i<p;i++)
        {
                for(j=0;j<q;j++)
                scanf("%d",&b[i][j]);
        }
```

```
        printf("\n The second matrix values are");
        for(i=0;i<p;i++)
        {
                printf("\n");
                for(j=0;j<q;j++)
                printf("%d", b[i][j]);
        }
        if(m==p&&n==q)
        {
                printf("\n Subtraction of two matrices is possible");
                printf("\n The resultant matrix values are");
                for(i=0;i<p;i++)
                {
                        printf("\n");
                        for(j=0;j<q;j++)
                        printf("%d", a[i][j]-b[i][j]);
                }
        }
        else
        printf("\n Subtraction of two matrices is not possible");
}
```

5. Given two matrices of order m×n and p×q respectively. Write a C program to find Multiplication of two matrices if possible otherwise display not possible.

```
#include<stdio. h>
void main()
{
        int a[10][10], m, n, i, j, b[10][10], p, q, c[10][10]={0}, k;
        printf(" enter order of first matrix");
        scanf("%d%d",&m,&n);
        printf("\n enter values in to first matrix");
        for(i=0;i<m;i++)
        {
```

```
        for(j=0;j<n;j++)
        scanf("%d",&a[i][j]);
}
printf("\n The first matrix values are");
for(i=0;i<m;i++)
{
        printf("\n");
        for(j=0;j<n;j++)
        printf("%d", a[i][j]);
}
printf(" enter order of second matrix");
scanf("%d%d",&p,&q);
printf("\n enter values in to second matrix");
for(i=0;i<p;i++)
{
        for(j=0;j<q;j++)
        scanf("%d",&b[i][j]);
}
printf("\n The second matrix values are");
for(i=0;i<p;i++)
{
        printf("\n");
        for(j=0;j<q;j++)
        printf("%d", b[i][j]);
}
if(n==p)
{
        printf("\n Multiplication of two matrices is possible");
        for(i=o;i<m;i++)
        {
                for(j=0;j<q;j++)
                {
                        for(k=0;k<n;k++)
                        c[i][j]+=a[i][k]*b[k][j];
```

```
                }
            }
            printf("\n The resultant matrix values are");
            for(i=0;i<m;i++)
            {
                printf("\n");
                for(j=0;j<q;j++)
                printf("%d", c[i][j]);
            }
        }
        else
        printf("\n Multiplication of two matrices is not possible");
}
```

Exercise:

1. Write a C program to count number of positive numbers, negative numbers, zeros in a matrix.
2. Write a C program to check whether the given matrix is symmetric matrix or not.
3. Write a C program to find sum of principal diagonal elements of a square matrix.
4. Write a C program to print upper triangular matrix, strictly upper triangular matrix of a given square matrix.
5. Write a C program to print lower triangular matrix, strictly lower triangular matrix of a given square matrix.

5.5 Multi Dimensional Arrays

If the array contains more than 2 index values then that arrays are called Multidimensional arrays.

Ex: 3d arrays

Syntax:

Datatype arrayname[index1][index2][index3];

Here index1 denotes plane size, index2 denotes row size and index3 denotes column size.

Ex: int a[1][2][3];

In the above example there is one plane with 2 rows and 3 columns.

Initialization:

Syntax: Datatype arrayname[index1][index2][index3]={value1, value2,.......};

Ex1: int a[1][2][2]={1, 2, 3, 4};

```
Ex2: int a[1][2][2]={
        {1, 2},
        {3, 4}
        };
```

Inputting the values into 3D array:

Ex: int a[2][3][4];

```
for(i=0;i<2;i++)
{
        for(j=0;j<3;j++)
        {
                for(k=0;k<4;k++)
                scanf("%d",&a[i][j][k]);
        }
}
```

Outputting the values of 3D array:

```
Ex: int a[2][3][4];
for(i=0;i<2;i++)
{ printf("\n");
        for(j=0;j<3;j++)
        {
                printf("\n");
                for(k=0;k<4;k++)
                printf("%d", a[i][j][k]);
        }
}
```

CHAPTER 6

Strings

6.1 Introduction

Group of characters or set of characters written under double quotes is called a string. String is nothing but character array in C language. A character can be an alphabet, digit or special symbol.

Ex:"ab","","$#@%","789"..... etc

In C, every string is ended or terminated by a special character called NULL character or '\0'

Declaration:

Syntax: datatype arrayname[array_size];

Ex: char A[10];

Initialization:

Storing the characters at the declaration of the string itself is called a String Initialization.

Syntax1: datatype arrayname[array_size]={'character1','character 2',...........};

Ex1: char a[4]={'a','b','c','\0'};

char a[4]={'a','b','\0'};

Note:

1. When number initialized character less than the size of the array remaining characters are automatically become NULL characters.
2. When string is initialized character by character, we have to store NULL character at the last.
3. When array size is 3, we can store only 2 original characters other than NULL character.

Syntax2: datatype arrayname[array_size]="characters";

Ex: char a[5]="siet";

's'	'i'	'e'	't'	'\0'
a[0]	a[1]	a[2]	a[3]	a[4]

Reading and Displaying a String:

Reading a String:

To read a string we can use either scanf() function or gets() function.

- Using scanf()

  Ex: char a[5];
  scanf("%s",&a);

- Note: scanf() function only reads a single word, but can't read multiple words if the string contains.

  Ex: char a[5];
  scanf("%s",&a);

  If we enter virat kohli as input the string a contains only virat but not virat kohli.

- To read a line of text, we use gets() function. gets() is an unformatted input function.

Syntax: gets(arrayname);
Ex: char a[5];
gets(a);

- To read a paragraph, we can use scanf() function with scan set.

  Ex: scanf("%[^\t]s", a);// it reads all lines of text till you press tab key.

Displaying a String:

To print or display a string or text, we can use either printf() function or puts() function.

Using printf():

Ex: printf(" the text is:%s", a);// %s is format specifier for a string or text, a is array name.

Using puts():

Syntax: puts(arrayname);
Ex: puts(a);

6.2 String Handling Functions or String Manipulation Functions

These are predefined functions available in string. h header file. These functions are used to manipulate or handle the strings. Some of the string handling functions are

- strlen()
- strcpy()
- strcat()
- strrev()
- strcmp()
- strlwr()
- strupr()
- strstr()

strlen(): This function gives the length of the string(number of characters in a string except NULL character will be counted).

Syntax: strlen(arrayname);

Ex: char a[4]="xy";
strlen(a); gives you the value 2.

strcpy(): This functions used copy the contents of one string into another string.

Syntax: strcpy(string2, string1);// here the contents of string1 copied to string2

Ex: char a[4]="xy", b[4];
strcpy(b, a);// then the b string contents are also "xy"

strcat():

This function used to join or combine the contents of one string at the end of another string.

Syntax: strcat(string2, string1);// here the contents of string1 joined at the end of to string2.

Ex: char a[4]="xy", b[4]="p";
strcat(b, a);// then the b string contents are also "pxy"

strrev():

This function reverses the contents of the given string.

Syntax: strrev(arrayname);

Ex: char a[4]="xy";
strrev(a);// gives you the result "yx"

strcmp():

This function used to compare one string with another character by character.

- If both strings are equal then strcmp() function gives zero otherwise it gives the ASCII value difference of first unmatched character in both strings.
- Syntax: strcmp(str1, str2);
- Ex 1: char str1[]="ab", str2[]="ab"; ASCII values A-Z is 65-90, a-z is 97-122, 0-9 is 48-57
  strcmp(str1, str2);-----0
- Ex 2: char str1[]="ab", str2[]="abab";
  strcmp(str1, str2);____ -97
- Ex3: char str1[]="abab", str2[]="ab";
  strcmp(str1, str2);-----97

strlwr():

This function converts all the upper case letters of a string into lower case letters.

- Ex: char str1[]="AB";
  strlwr(str1);-----ab

strupr():

This function converts all the lower case letters of a string into upper case letters.

- Ex: char str1[]="ab";
  strupr(str1);----- AB

strstr():

This function searches a sub string in a main string and it gives a non zero value if its found otherwise NULL.

Syntax: strstr(str1, str2);// here str1 is main string and str2 is sub string

- Ex: char a[4]="ab", b[4]="c";
  strstr(a, b)----output->NULL

Programs:

1. Write a C program to find the length of a string without using string handling functions.

```
#include<stdio. h>
#include<string. h>
void main()
{
        char a[10];
        int i;
        printf(" enter a string");
        gets(a);
        i=0;
        while(a[i]!='\0')
        i++;
        printf("\n The length of the given string %s is %d", a, i);
}
```

2. Write a C program to check whether the given string is palindrome string or not using string handling functions.

```
#include<stdio. h>
#include<string. h>
void main()
{
        char a[10], b[10];
        printf(" enter a string");
        gets(a);
        strcpy(b, a);
        strrev(b);
        if(strcmp(a, b)==0)
        printf("\n given string %s is a palindrome", a);
        else
        printf("\n given string %s is not a palindrome", a);
}
```

3. Write a C program to check whether the given string is palindrome string or not without using string handling functions.

```
#include<stdio. h>
#include<string. h>
void main()
{
        char a[10];
        int i, n;
        printf(" enter a string");
        gets(a);
        i=0;
        while(a[i]!='\0')
        i++;
        n=i;
        for(i=0;a[i]!='\0';i++)
        {
                if(a[i]!=a[n-1-i])
                break;
                else
                continue;
        }
        if(i<n)
        printf("\n given string %s is a palindrome", a);
        else
        printf("\n given string %s is not a palindrome", a);
}
```

4. Write a C program to insert a substring into a main string at a particular position.

```
#include<stdio. h>
#include<string. h>
void main()
{
```

```
        char a[50], b[10], c[100];
        int i, p, j;
        printf(" enter a main string");
        gets(a);
        printf("\n enter a substring");
        gets(b);
        printf("\n enter position of main string to insert substring");
        scanf("%d",&p;
        for(i=0, j=0;i<p;i++)
        c[j++]=a[i++];
        for(i=0;b[i]!='\0';i++)
        c[j++]=b[i++];
        for(i=p;a[i]!='\0';i++)
        c[j++]=b[i++];
        c[j]='\0';
        printf("\n after inserting substring %s in main string %s at
        position %d is %s", b, a, p, c);
}
```

5. Write a C program to find number of characters, number of lines and number of words in a paragraph.

```
#include<stdio. h>
#include<string. h>
void main()
{
        char a[100];
        int i, noc=0, now=nol=1;
        printf(" enter a paragraph, press tab key to stop entering");
        scanf("%[^\t]s",&a);
        for(i=0;a[i]!='\0';i++)
        {
                noc++;
                If (a[i]==' '||a[i]=='\n')
                now++;
```

```
            if(a[i]=='\n')
            nol++;
    }
    printf("\n The paragraph contains %d number of characters,%d
    number of words,%d number of lines", noc, now, nol);
}
```

Exercise:

1. Write a C program to read a paragraph and character and find the occurences of that character in the paragraph.
2. Write a C program to read a paragraph, character and substring. Replace all the occurences of that character in the paragraph with substring.
3. Write a C program to find third most frequently occurred character in a given paragraph.
4. Write a C program to check whether the given two strings are anagrams or not.
5. Write a C program to count number of vowels, special symbol '@' in a paragraph.

6.3 Array of Strings or Table of Strings

Declaration: datatype arrayname[index1][index2];

Index1 indicates number of strings and index2 indicates size of each string

Ex: char a[10][30];// there are 10 strings with length 30 characters.

Reading Table of strings:

We can use gets() function for this.

```
Ex: char a[10][30];
for(i=0;i<10;i++)
gets(a[i]);
```

Displaying Table of strings:

We can use puts() function for this.

```
Ex: char a[10][30];
for(i=0;i<10;i++)
puts(a[i]);
```

Program:

Write a C program to read n number of names of your class and display those names in alphabetical order.

```
#include<stdio. h>
#include<string. h>
void main()
{
        char a[100][30], t[40];
        int i, j, n;
        printf(" how many names you want to enter");
        scanf("%d",&n);
        printf("\n enter %d names", n);
        for(i=0;i<n;i++)
        gets(a[i]);
        printf("\n the entered names are");
        for(i=0;i<n;i++)
        printf("\n%s", a[i]);
        for(i=1;i<n;i++)
        {
                for(j=0;j<n;j++)
        {
        if(strcmp(a[j], a[j+1])>0)
        {
                strcpy(t, a[j]);
                strcpy(a[j], a[j+1]);
```

```
            strcpy(a[j+1], t);
            }
    }
    printf("\n the entered names in alphabetical order are");
    for(i=0;i<n;i++)
    printf("\n%s", a[i]);
}
```

CHAPTER 7

Functions

7.1 Introduction

So far we have written programs to solve a small problems. When we want to solve a large or complex problems, our program may contain more statements means the length of the program (size of the program) increases. This causes the following drawbacks

Drawbacks or Disadvantages:

- Program size is big (number of statements are more).
- Understanding of the program logic is difficult.
- Identifying the mistakes in the program also difficult.
- Same code of the program (statements) may be repeated.

To overcome the above drawbacks, instead of writing a big program for large or complex problems. We divide the actual program into sub programs. The process of dividing the program in to subprograms is called ***modularization*** and this approach is called ***Top down approach***.

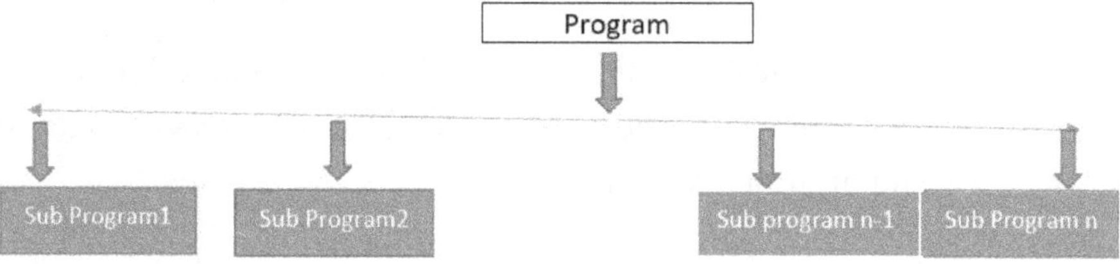

SUB PROGRAM OR FUNCTION:

Sub program is called as ***Function or Module***.

Function: it contains group of statements to solve a problem. Functions are ***two types***

- Standard functions
- User defined functions.

Standard Functions: These functions are already available in the header files. These functions are also called library functions, system defined functions or built in functions.

Examples:

- printf (), scanf() –these are standard output and input functions available in stdio. h
- sqrt(), pow() –these are mathematical functions available in math. h

User defined functions: These functions are created or defined by the user to solve a problem. User can create or define own functions to solve the problems.

Examples:

- main () –It is a function which also the user to write statements to solve theproblem. That is why main () is called user defined function.
- Myfunction () - user can create a function like Myfucntion ().

Characteristics or properties of User defined Functions:

- Every function has uniquely identified by a name i. e. called function name followedby parenthesis (or brackets ()) with or without arguments or parameters.

- Example: main ()- it is a function. Here main is a function name and it has no arguments or parameters in the parenthesis.
- fun(a, b);- Here a, b are called arguments or parameters.

Note: we follow the rules of writing the identifiers for writing the function names also.

- In C language every function returns one kind of value. The default return value of any function is integer value.

  Examples:

  - ```
    int main()
    {
    - -
    - -
    return 0;
    }
    ```
  - ```
    float average()
    {
    - - -
    - - -
    return x;
    }
    ```

- Every Function has Function declaration, function call and function definition.
- Every function gets activated when it is called by other function or functions.

Advantages of User Defined Functions:

- Program size becomes small.
- Understanding the logic of a Program is easy.
- Debugging (identifying the mistakes) process becomes easy.

- Duplication of the code (redundancy of the code) is avoided or eliminated.
- Reusability of the code is possible means we write the function once and that function can be used any number of times.

7.2 Function Declaration or Function Prototype

This gives basic information about the function.

Syntax:

returndatatype functionname (parameter or argument list);

functionname: it is a valid name (should follow the naming rules of an identifier) for identification of a function.

returndatatype: it denotes the type of value returned or gives back by the function. The return datatype can be an **int, char, float** ...

parameter or argument list: it denotes the type of values received by the function. This list contains variables along with datatypes.

Example:

1. int add(int a, int b);
   Here add is a function name, int is a return data type of a function and int a, int b are called parameter or argument list.
2. void vmeg_hyd();
   Here vmeg_hyd is a function name, void is a return data type without parameters or parameter list.

7.3 Calling Function and Called Function

The function which calls another function is called as *calling function.*

The function which is called by calling function is called as *Called function.*

Example:

```
void f ( )
{
        ----- g ( );
        ---------
}
void   g (     )
{
        -----
        -----
        -----
        --------
}
```

Here f() is called as calling function and g() is called as called function.

7.4 Function Call

Function gets invoked when it is called. To use the function we have to call that function. We can call the function many ways. Some ways are

1. Using function name.
   Example: add ();
2. using function name with parameters(only variables or constants)
   Example: add (5, 6, 7);
   Sub (a, b);

7.5 Return Statement

In C language, every function returns one kind of value by using return statement. return statement available in various forms.

- return;
  It means return statement is not returning any value.(it returns nothing).

- Syntax:
  return variable or constant;
  Example: return 9;
  return 1. 7;
  return 'n';
  return p;// here p can be any type of variable.
  return 5, 2, 7, 3;// we won't get any error but only the first value returned remaining values are omitted.
- Syntax:
  return expression;
  Example:
  a. return 9-5+6;// here first the expression will be solved then that value will be returned.
  b. return a+b;
  c. return a-9+b*c/d*4;

7.6 Function Definition

It gives more information about a solution of a problem separately. Syntax:

returndatatype functionname(parameter list) ⟶ function header

```
{Statement 1;
        Statement 2;
        -----
        Statement n;
}
```

⟶ function body

functionname: it is a valid name (should follow the naming rules of an identifier) for identification of a function.

returndatatype: it denotes the type of value returned or gives back by the function. The return datatype can be an **int, char, float** ...

parameter or argument list: it denotes the type of values received by the function. This list contains variables along with datatypes.

Function Body: it contains group of statements to solve a problem.

Example:

i.
```
int add (int a, int b)
{
        int c;
        c=a+b; return c;
}
```

Here add is a function name, int is a return data type of a function and int a, int b are called parameter or argument list.

ii.
```
void vmeg_hyd()
{
        Int a, b;
        printf(" enter a, b");
        scanf("%d%d",&a,&b); printf("\n sum =%d", a+b);
}
```

7.7 Actual Arguments and Formal Arguments

The arguments that are specified at calling a function are called Actual arguments and the arguments that are specified at called function are called formal arguments. Arguments are called Parameters.

Example:

```
void    f()// calling function
{
        G(p);// calling function G()
}
void G(int A)  // called function
{
        ----
```

}

In the Above example f () is called as calling function G () is called as called function and p is called as actual argument and A is called as formal argument.

Note:

- Function Declaration or prototype should be written before main () function i. e. in the global declaration area.
- Function call statement should be written with in the main () function generally.
- Function definition can be written before or after main ( ) function.

7.8 Types of Functions Based on Return Value

User defined functions are two types based on return value.

1. Void functions
2. Non void functions

   Void functions: Functions that don't return any value are said to be Void functions. Example: void main()

   {

   }

   Non void functions: Functions that return any value are said to be non-Void functions. Example:

   Int main()

   {

```
        ---
return 0;
}
```

7.9 Categories of User Defined Functions or Basic Function Design Techniques

Based on return values and parameters, user defined functions are divided in to four types.

1. void function without parameters (or) function with no return value and with no parameters.
2. Void function with parameters (or) function with no return value and with parameters.
3. Non void function without parameters (or) function with return value and with no parameters.
4. Non void function with parameters (or) function with return value and with parameters.

1. void function without parameters:

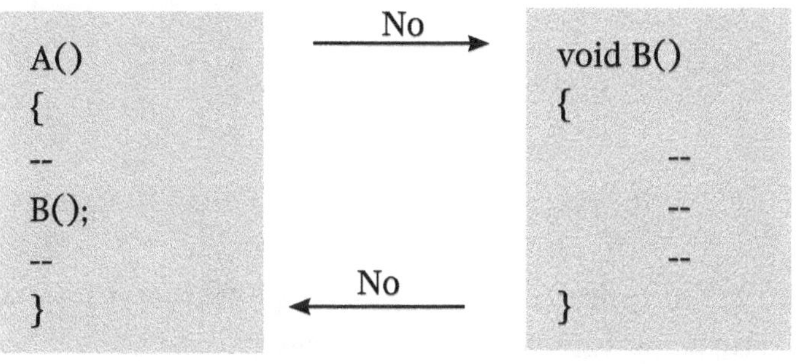

Calling function Called function

In this the called function does not receive any value from calling function and it does not return any value to calling function.

Example: C program to add two numbers using void function without parameters. void add();// function declaration or prototype

```
void main()
{
        add();//function call
}
void add()// function definition
        {
                int a, b;
                printf("enter a, b");
                scanf("%d%d",&a,&b);
                printf("\n sum value=%d", a+b);
        }
```

1. Void function with parameters:

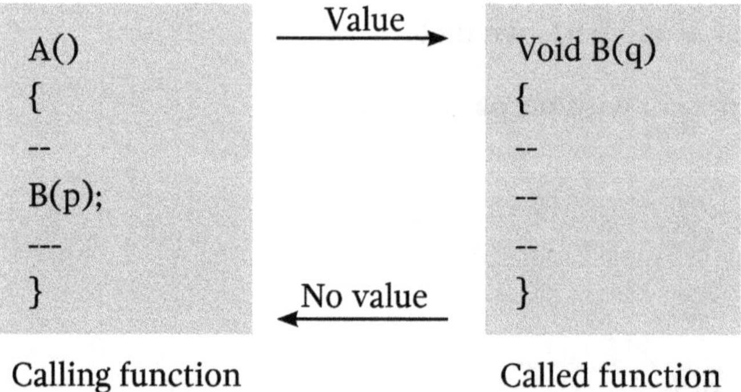

In this the called function receives value from calling function and it does not return any value to calling function.

Example: C program to add two numbers using void function without parameters.

```
void add(int a, int b);// function declaration or prototype
void main()
{
        int a, b;
        printf("enter a, b");
        scanf("%d%d",&a,&b); add(a, b);//function call
}
void add(int a, int b)// function definition
{
        printf("\n sum value=%d", a+b);
}
```

2. Non void function without parameters:

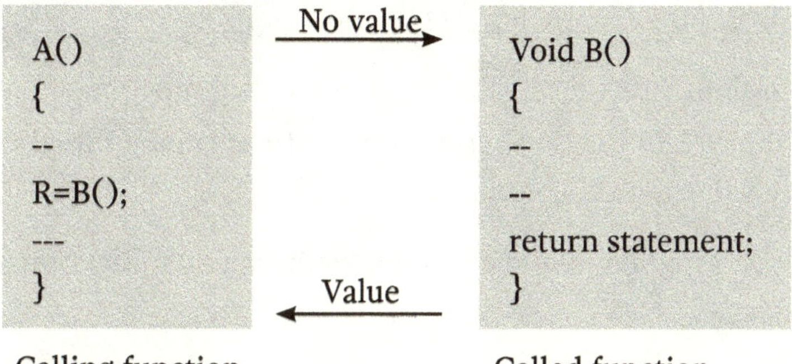

Calling function Called function

In this the called function receives no value from calling function and it returns a value to calling function.

Example: C program to add two numbers using void function without parameters.

```
int add();// function declaration or prototype
void main()
{ int r;
r= add();//function call
printf("\n sum value=%d", r);
}
```

```
int add()// function definition
{
        printf("enter a, b");
        scanf("%d%d",&a,&b); return a+b;
}
```

3. Non void function with parameters:

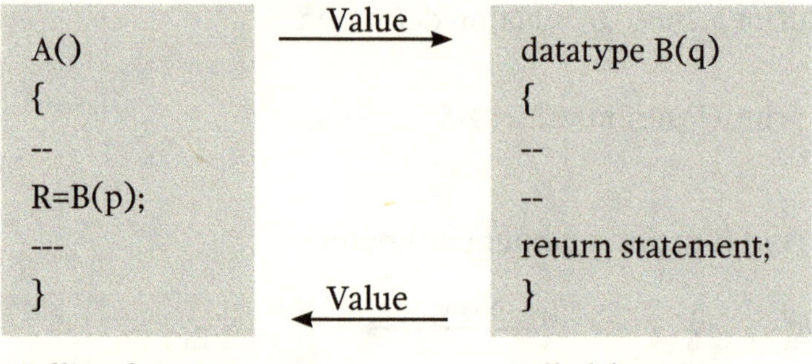

Calling function Called function

In this the called function receives value from calling function and it returns a value to calling function.

Example: C program to add two numbers using void function without parameters.

```
int add(int a, int b);// function declaration or prototype
void main()
{ int r, a, b;
printf("enter a, b");
scanf("%d%d",&a,&b); r= add(a, b);//function call
printf("\n sum value=%d", r);
}
int add(int a, int b)// function definition
{
        return a+b;
}
```

Programs on user defined functions:

1. C program to find factorial of a number using function.

```
#include<stdio. h>
long int factorial(int n); void main()
{
        int nr;
        long int r;
        printf("enter a number");
        scanf("%d",&nr);
        r=factorial(n);
        printf("\n factorial of number %d is %ld", nr, r);
}
long int factorial(int n)
{
        int i;
        long int fa=1;
        for(i=1;i<=n;i++)
        fa=fa*i;
        return fa;
}
```

2. C program to find nth term in a Fibonacci series using function.

```
#include<stdio. h>
int fibo(int n); void main()
{
        int n, r;
        printf("enter a number");
        scanf("%d",&n); r=fibo(n);
        printf("\n Fibonacci term value is %d", r);
}
int fibo(int n)
{
        int i, a=0, b=1, c;
```

```
        if(n==1)
        return 0; else
        if(n==2)
        return 1; else
        {
                for(i=3;i<=n;i++)
                {
                        c=a+b;
                        a=b;
                        b=c;
                }
        return c;
        }
}
```

3. Write a C program to find reverse of a given number.

```
int reverse(int n);
void main()
{
        int n, r;
        printf("\n enter a number");
        scanf("%d",&n);
        r=reverse(n);
        printf("\n reverse of %d is %d", n, r);
}
Int reverse(int n)
{
        int d, rev=0;
        while(n!=0)
        {
                d=n%10;
                rev=rev*10+d;
                n/=10;
        }
```

```
        return rev;
}
```

Exercise:

1. Write a C program to find sum of the digits of a number using functions.
2. Write a C program to check whether the given number is palindrome number or not using functions.
3. Write a C program to check whether the given number is prime number or not using functions.
4. Write a C program to check whether the given number is perfect number or not using functions.
5. Write a C program to check whether the given number is Armstrong number or not using functions.

7.10 Parameter Passing Techniques or Inter Function Communication Techniques

Parameter Passing Techniques are used to establish the communication between functions through arguments. Parameter Passing Techniques are two types

call by value

call by reference.

Call by Value or Pass by value:

This mechanism or technique or procedure works as follows

- The method of passing arguments from calling function to called function by value or values is called call by value or pass by value mechanism.
- During function call execution, the values or value of actual arguments will be copied to formal arguments.

- If any changes made to the values of formal arguments or parameters those changes will not affect the values of actual arguments or parameters.

```
#include<stdio. h>
void myswap(int ia, int ib);
void main()
{
        int ix=100, iy=50; myswap(x, y);
        printf("\n In main function, ix value=%i, iy value=%i", ix, iy);
}
        void myswap (int ia, int ib)
{
        int it; it=ia;
        ia=ib;
        ib=it;
        printf ("\n In swap function, ia value=%i, ib value=%i", ia, ib);
}
```

Output:

In swap function, ia value=50, ib value =100
In main function, ix value=100, iy value =50

Explanation:

In the above myswap program the initial values of variables are ix=100 and iy=50. These are passed as parameters to called function myswap() from calling function. user defined unction myswap() has formal parameters ia and ib equivalent of ix and iy variable names and this code exchanges the values of variables. After swapping the flow control comes back to main( ) function, but the values of variables are not changed or not updated in the main( ) function.

7.11 Recursion

Recursion is the procedure or method of calling a function to itself to solve small problems which can be expressed their solution interms of itself by reducing the problem size is called recursion.

Recursive Function: If a function makes a call to itself then it is called Recursive function.

Characteristics:

- Every Recursive function has two parts –***base case and recursive case.***
  - **Base case**: it is a statement that denotes stopping point of recursion process. It also gives direct solution to the problem.
  - ***Recursive case:*** it is a statement that denotes solution to a problem can be expressed in terms of itself.
- Recursive functions can be used for the implementation of various linear data structures like linked lists and non linear data structures like trees, graphs.
- Example to find factorial of a given number using recursion or recursive function

  Assume given number is n

  According to mathematics n!=nxn-1xn-2......x2x1

  We can write the same formula like this also

  n!=nx(n-1)!

  The solution of a factorial of a given number can be expressed interms of base case and recursive case

  n!= 1 if n=0// This is called base case

  nx(n-1)!//This is called recursive case

Programs based on recursive functions:

1. Write a C program to find the factorial value of a input number using recursive function

```
// C program to find the factorial value of a input number using recursive function

#include <stdio. h>
unsigned long int rfact(int nr);
void main( )
{
        unsigned long int fa;
        int nr;
        printf("enter a number to find factorial \n");
        scanf("%i",&nr);
        fa=rfact(nr);
        printf("factorial value of given number %d is %ld", nr, fa);
}
unsigned long int rfact(int ac)
{
        if(ac==0)// base case
        return 1;
        else
        return ac*fact(ac-1);//recursive case
}
```

Output:
enter a number to find factorial: 1
factorial value of given number 1 is1
enter a number to find factorial:
2 factorial value of given number 2 is2

2. Write a C program to find n^{th} Fibonacci term using recursion.

```
#include<stdio. h>
int fibo(int n); void main()
{
        int n;;
        printf("\n enter term number");
        scanf("%d",&n);
        r=f ibo(n);
        printf("\n term value=%d", r);
}
int fibo(int n)
{
        if(n==1) return 0;
        else if(n==2) return 1; else
        return fibo(n-1)+fibo(n-2);
}
```

3. Write a C program to find nth Fibonacci term using recursion.

```
#include<stdio. h>
int reverse(int n);
int rev=0;// global variable void main()
{
        int n;
        printf("\n enter term number");
        scanf("%d",&n);
        r=reverse(n);
        printf("\n term value=%d", r);
}
int reverse(int n)
{
        int d; if(n==0) return ; else
        {
                d =n%10;
```

```
            rev=rev*10+d; reverse(n/10);
    }
return rev;
}
```

Exercise:

1. Write a C program to find XY using recursion(Y can be positive or negative).
2. Write a C program to find gcd of two positive numbers.
3. Write a C program to find multiplication of two numbers using recursion.
4. Write a C program to implement the following function using recursion F(n)= 2 if n=1
   2*f(n-1) if n>1
5. Write a C program to implement the following function using recursion A(m, n)= n+1 if m=0
   A(m-1, 1) if m>0 and n=0
   A(m-1, A(m, n-1)) if m>0 and n>0

6. Find the output of the following code

```
#include <stdio. h>
int fun(int n)
{
        if (n == 4) return n;
        else return 2*fun(n+1);
}
int main()
{
        printf("%d ", fun(2));
        return 0;
}
```

7. Consider the following recursive function fun(x, y). What is the value of fun(4, 3)?

```
int fun(int x, int y)
{
        if (x == 0) return y;
        return fun(x - 1, x + y);
}
```

7.12 Storage Classes in C

This concept gives four kinds of information about the variables. They are

Storage or storage area: it is a place where the variables are stored. Generally variables are stored either in main memory or cpu registers.

Default value: it specify the value of a variable at the declaration or initial value of the variable.

Scope: it specify in which region or area a variable can be used.

Life time: how long the value of a variable is available in the memory for usage during program execution is specified by life time.

C language has four different kinds of storage classes namely

1. Auto storage class
2. Static storage class
3. Extern storage class
4. Register storage class

1. Auto storage class:

These are also called Local variables or Automatic Variables. These variables are defined within a function or block and they are produced when the block/function is executed and ruined/vanished when the function execution is over or flow control comes out of the block.

The keyword ***auto*** used for Auto storage class name.

Syntax;

Storageclassname datatype variableName ;

Example:

1. auto int ax;// here ax is automatic variable
2. int bx;// here bx is automatic variable even though no storage class is specified

Characterstics:

Storage area: main memory
Default Value: unknown
Scope: it's limited to a block or function in which they are declared.
Lifetime: the value of a variable is available in the memory for usage as long as the flow control in that region or area.

Example:

```
void main( )
{
        int ix=10;
        printf("%i"i, x);
        {
                auto int iy=20;
                printf("%i %i"i, x, iy);
        }
        printf("%i %i", ix, iy);//error
}
```

2. Static storage class:

Throughout or entire the program value of these variables are active. At the time of declaration, static variable can be initialized only one time. The execution of initialization statement happens only one time and persists the value of a variable untill the program execution is over.

The keyword ***static*** used for *Static* storage class name.

Syntax;

Storageclassname datatype variableName ;

Example:

static int ax;// here ax is static variable
int bx;// here bx is automatic variable even though no storage class is specified

Characterstics:

Storage area: main memory
Default Value: zero
Scope: it's limited to a block or function in which they are declared.
Lifetime: the value of a static variable is available in the memory for usage as long as the program is running.

Example:

```
void gf();
void main()
{
        gf();
        gf();
}
void gf()
{
        static int x;
        printf("%d ", x); x=x+10;
}
```

Output:

0
10

3. Extern storage class:

These are also called External variables or global variables. These can be declared or defined either before or after a function. During running of declaration statement, memory will be reserved and is not ruined when the controlflow comes out of the function to go to another function.

The keyword ***extern*** used for *Extern* storage class name.

Syntax:

Storageclassname datatype variableName ;

Example:

extern int ax;// here ax is static variable

Characterstics:

Storage area: main memory
Default Value: zero
Scope: any where with in a file or between the files.
Lifetime: the value of a static variable is available in the memory for usage as long as the program is running.

Example:

```
void f();
int x;
void main()
{
        f();
        printf("In main function x=%d", x); f();
}
void f()
{
        printf("%d ", x);
        x=x+10;
}
```

Output:

0
In main function x=10
10

4. Register storage class:

These are also called register variables. These are useful only

- when any variable is used iteratively in a program.
- When main memory is not sufficient.
- To access the data quickly.

The keyword ***register*** used for register storage class name.

Syntax:

Storageclassname datatype variableName ;

Example:

1. register int ax;// here ax is automatic variable
2. int bx;// here bx is automatic variable even though no storage class is specified

Characterstics:

Storage area: cpu registers
Default Value: unknown
Scope: it's limited to a block or function in which they are declared.
Lifetime: the value of a variable is available in the memory for usage as long as the flow control in that region or area.

Example:

```
void main()
{
        register int ix, iy;
        printf("\n enter ix, iy");
```

```
    scanf("%d%d",&ix,&iy);// error
    printf("\n sum=%d", x+y);
}
```

CHAPTER 8

Pointers

8.1 Introduction

One of thevbasic concepts of C is Pointers. It is a derived data type. C programming language has basic data types like int, char, float, doule, void and this can be derived from those.

The benefits of pointer concept in C are as follows

- few calculations can done trough pointers only.
- It reduces the program size.
- To solve difficult problems.
- To access the data quickly.
- Arrays and tables of data can be handled effectively and efficiently
- Dynamic memory allocation can be achieved
- Data can be communicated between the functions
- implementation of linear, non linear data structures is possible.

8.2 Basics

Consider the following variables declared in a program:

```
char n;
int num;
float ht;
```

When a variable is declared the compiler allocates some memory and address for the it. Assume character one byte, float four bytes and int two bytes are reserved. The following diagram illustrates how the above declared variables might be arranged in memory along with their addresses.

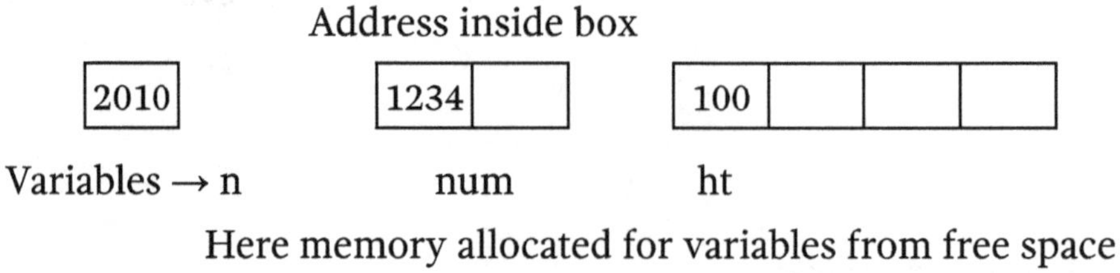

Address inside box

2010		1234			100			

Variables → n num ht

Here memory allocated for variables from free space

8.3 Pointer Definition

A pointer is a special variable that holds/stores the address of another variable of same data type. Another variable could be anythinga. Data type could be a float, int, char, double, etc.

Consider the following example statement:

char num =10;

For character variable, assume the address of the character variable is 100.

This can be diagrammatically represented as below.

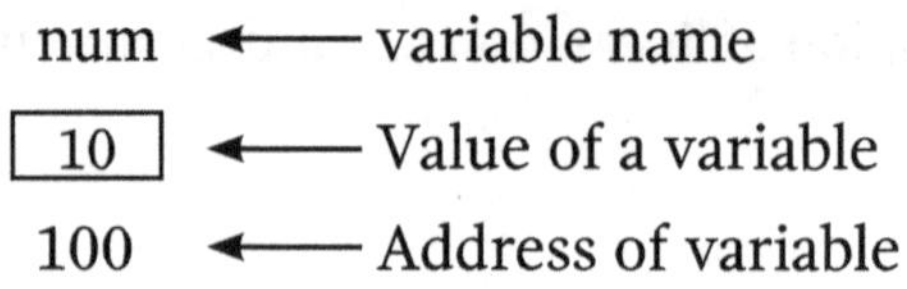

num ⟵ variable name

| 10 | ⟵ Value of a variable

100 ⟵ Address of variable

During the execution of program computer always associates the character variable num with address 100. The value 10 can be accessed by using either the variable number or the address of it which is 100. Since memory addresses are simply numbers they can be assigned to some variables which can be stored in memory like any other variables. Such variables that hold memory addresses are called as 'pointer variables' the pointer variable is nothing but a variable that contains an address of another variable in memory. When a pointer contains address of integer variable, such pointer is called *integer pointer*. Similarly float, char pointers contain the address of char and float data type.

8.4 Declaration

In C every variable must be declared before it is used. Since pointer is a special variable, its declaration is also different. An operator called dereference operator or indirection operator is used to declare a Pointer. It is represented by *(asterisk). The '*' symbol appears in C language in four different situations with four different meanings.

Two of these are well known.

i. Comments/*...*/
ii. Arithmetic operator for multiplication as in a*b
iii. Declaring pointer variable using *(dereference operator)

Usage of deference operator in comment can be easily recognized. Multiplication needs two operands; this can also be easily recognized. When it appears in a declaration as int *p, read it is read as p is a pointer to an integer. The syntax of pointer declarations

data-type *variable-name;

Here data type can be int, float, char etc and the dereference operator before the int variable variable-name tells that it is a pointer variable. Hence the pointer variable variable-name holds the address of another variable of the same data type. For example,

A pointer is declared by assigning an asterisk (*) in front of the variable name in the declaration statement.

```
int x;
int *pt;// pt is a pointer to integer
char *q;//q is a pointer to character.
```

The “dereferencing operator” the asterisk can also be is used as follows:

```
*pt = 70;
```

This will copy 70 to the address pointed to by **pt**. Thus if **pt** “points to” (contains the address of) **x**, the above statement will set the value of x to 70. That is, when the ‘*’ is used this way, it is referring to the value of that which ptr is pointing to, not the value of the pointer itself.

Pointer Declaration Styles

The dereference operator (*) can appear anywhere between the data type name and the pointer variable name as shown below

```
int * pt;//type1 between the data type and variable
int *pt;//type 2 Close to varible
int* pt;//type 3 close to data type
```

Multiple Declarations

Multiple pointers of same data type can be declared as given below.

```
char *pt, xt, *qt;
```

Here pt and qt are pointer variables and xt is character variable.

8.5 Pointer Initialization

Consider the declaration

```
int ii, jj,*pp;
```

- It declares a pointer variable p that can point to an integer. Just this kind of declaration, doesn’t specify where a integer pointer pp has to point at particular. In other words it does not say anything about which particular integer variable address it has to hold, either of int ii or of int jj, in this case. To explicitly specify where variable a pointer has to point to, a unary operator called *reference or address operator (&) is* used. The reference operator (&) cannot be applied to expressions, constants, or register variables. To initialize the pointer variable reference operator (&) is used with pointer variable. To understand different types of initialization consider the following examples,

```
float ii, jj,*pp;
pp = &ii;
```

This causes p pointer variable to point at i the integer data type. Here

- * is the *indirection* operator
- & is the *address* operator

The Address of Variables

All the variables that are declared in programs are allocated addresses in the memory. This address can be printed out using the & operator. (which has already been used in scanf(). For example, consider the below program.

```
#include <stdio. h>
void main()
{
        int x;
        x=1;
        printf(" %d", x);
        printf("\n %d", &x);
}
```

OUTPUT:

```
1
63591
```

Explanation:

In this case, the value will be stored in 4 locations, not one, since integer requires 2 bytes to store. However 1 is 'sliced' into 2 parts Here, what is the address of x? Actually it is 63591, 63592. However in C we consider the address as 63591, the address of first of the two locations. This is an important thing to remember and crucial to the understanding of pointers concept.

```
float xx;
float *ptr;
ptr=&x;// Address of x is assigned to pointer variable
*ptr=x;// The value of x is assigned to ptr
```

8.5 Null Pointers

A pointer is said to be a null pointer when its value is 0. Remember, a null pointer can never point to valid data. To set a null pointer, simply assign 0 to the pointer variable. Forexample:

```
char *pc; int *pt; pt=pc=0;
```

Here pt and pc pointers become null pointers after the integer value of 0 is assigned to them. Later in the program any required value can be assigned to null pointers. This analogous to initializing the variables to zero value in the program, such as

```
int x=0; X=5;
```

Understanding pointers

Pointers have the following two important aspects. They are given below. &x = address of variablex.

*p = content of address given by p.

Pointers concept is well understood by following example problems.

1. Write a program to display the contents of apointer.

```
#include <stdio. h>
void main( )
{
        int x = 34;
        int *ptr;
        ptr =&x;
        printf("Address of x: 0x%p\n", ptr);
        printf("Address of x: 0x%x\n", &x);
        printf("Address of ptr: 0x%x\n", &ptr);
        printf("Value of x: %d\n", *ptr);
}
```

Output:

```
Address of x: 0xFACE
Address of x: 0Xbee5
Address of ptr: 0xfaceb
Value of x: 34
```

Note: Format specifiers %x,%X and %p are used to get the address of the variable in c. ox in the address refers that the format of address is in hexadecimal format.

%x -> Hexadecimal value represented with lowercase characters (unsigned integer type)

%X -> Hexadecimal value represented with uppercase characters (unsigned integer type)

%p -> Displays a memory addresses (pointer type) compatible to the computer memory.

2. Write a simple program to understand the usage deference and reference operators in pointers

```
#include <stdio. h>
void main()
{
        int *ntr, qg;
        qg = 23;
        ntr = &qg;
        printf(" %d ", qg);
        printf("\n %d ",*ntr);
        printf("%u ", ntr);
}
```

OUTPUT

```
23
23
321123
```

8.6 Pointer Expressions

To understand the working of pointers consider the below expressions.

```
int xx, yy;
int *pr1,*pr2;
```

1. pr1=&xx;
   The memory address of the variable xx is assigned to pointer variable pr1.
2. yy=*pr1
   pointer variable pr1 is holding the address. The value of that address is assigned to the variable yy, not the memory address.
3. pr1=&xx; pr2=ptr1;
   pr1 holds the address of the variable due to first declaration. In the second declaration content of pr1 is the address ofx x

is transferred to pr2. Hence both pr1, pr2 both will be holding the same address.

4. For good understanding of the pointers, consider some of the invalid declarations given below.

   i. int xx;
      int p1; p1=&x;

   Error: pointer declaration must have the prefix of dereference (*) operator.

   ii. float x;
       float *v;v=x;

   Error: While assigning variable to the pointer variable the address operator (&) must be used along with thevariable.

   iii. int xx;
        char *n; n=&xx;

   Error: Mixing of data type is not allowed.

8.7 Pointer Arithmetic

Addirion, subtraction, multiplication, division, modulus division are called arithmetic operations. but all arithmetic oerations can't be applicable on pointers. The supported operations are

Addition
subtraction
Pointer increment
Pointer decrement

Pointer increment and decrement

Integer, float, char, double data type pointers can be incremented and decremented. For all these data types both prefix and post fix increment

or decrement is allowed. Integer pointers are incremented or decremented in the multiples of two. Similarly character by one, float by four and double pointers by eight etc.

Let int*p;

```
P++    //valid
++p    //valid
p--    //valid
--p    //valid
```

This is illustrated in the below program.

```
#include <stdio. h>
void main()
{
        int *p1, p;
        float *f1, f;
        char *c1, c;
        p1=&p; f1=&f; c1=&c;
        printf("Memory address before increment:\n int=%p\n,
        float=%p\n, char=%p\n", p1, f1, c1);
        p1++;
        f1++;
        c1++;
        printf("Memory address after increment:\n int=%p\n,
        float=%p\n, char=%p\n", p1, f1, c1);
}
```

Output:

```
Memory address before increment: int=0044BB18  //int  Occupies
twobytes
          float=0076AF3B     //float occupies four bytes
          char=0076AF3E      //character occupies onebyte
Memory address after increment: int=0045AF1B
          float=0045AF2F
          char=0045AF3F
```

8.7.1 Pointer Addition and Subtraction

Other than addition and subtraction, no other operations are allowed on integer pointers. Addition and subtraction with float or double data type pointers are not allowed. Pointers cannot be added or subtracted from each other. For example,

```
float *ptr1,*ptr2;
ptr1=ptr1+ptr2;// invalid
ptr1=ptr1-ptr2;/* invalid */
```

A fixed value can be added or subtracted from integer pointer variable.

For example,

```
int *p; p=p+6;, p=p-3;
```

8.7.2 Pointer Multiplication and Division

Multiplication or division is not allowed with the pointers.

Example:

```
int *pr1,*pr2;
pr1=pr1*pr2;//Invalid
pr1=pr1/pr2;//Invalid
```

Pointer cannot be multiplied or divided a pointer by value.

Example:

```
ptr = ptr * 2;// invalid
ptr = ptr/3;// invalid
```

8.8 Pointers and Functions

Call by Reference Mechanism or Pass by reference Mechanism:
This mechanism or technique or procedure works as follows

- The method of passing arguments from calling function to called function by address or addresses is called call by reference or pass by reference mechanism.

- During function call execution, the address or addresses of actual arguments will be copied to formal arguments.
- If any changes made to the values of formal arguments or parameters those changes will affect the values of actual arguments or parameters.

```
#include<stdio. h>
void myswap(int *ia, int *ib);
void main()
{
        int ix=100, iy=50; myswap(&ix,&iy);
        printf("\n In main function, ix value=%i, iy value=%i", ix, iy);
}
void myswap (int *a, int *b)
{
        int it; it=*a;*a=*b;
        *b=it;
        printf ("\n In swap function, a value=%i, b value=%i",*a,*b);
}
```

Output:

In swap function, a value=50, b value =100
In main function, ix value=50, iy value =1000

8.9 Pointers and Arrays

An array is actually very much like a pointer. We can declare the arrays first element of array can be declared as a1[0] or as int *a1 because a[0] is an address and *a is also an address.

8.9.1 Pointers and One Dimensional Array

An array is a collection of items of the same data type. For example, the following are all array declarations:

```
int xx[20];// an array of integers
char n[30];// an array of characters
double ga1[10];// an array of doubles
```

Consider the following:

```
int xx[5] = {8, 4, 9, 6};
```

Here array xx is containing 4 integers. Each of these integers can be referred by means of a subscript to xx i. e. using xx**[0]** through xx**[3]**. Alternatively array can be access ed via a pointer as follows:

```
int *pp;        //declare the pointer
pp=&xx[0];      // pointer points to first element of the array
```

In the similar way other array elements can also be accessed as given below.

```
pp = &xx[1];// pointer points to second element of the array
pp=&xx[2];//pointer points to third element of the array
pp = &xx[3];//pointer points to fourth element of the array
```

The other way of assigning the array to pointer is

```
int pt[200]; int*ptrp; ptrp=pt;
```

This is exactly same as ptrp=pt[0];

The following equalities are also valid. Ptrp+3=&pt[3];

```
*ptrp==&pt[0];
*(ptrp+3)==&pt[3];
```

The array subscripting is defined in terms of pointer arithmetic. The expression a[i]is defined to be same as *(a+i).

Array and pointers concept can be well understood by the following program.

```
#include<stdio. h>
void main()
{
```

```
        int aa[4]={11, 12, 13, 14};
        int*ptrp;
        int ip, np, tempp; np=14;
        Printf(" \n array values are") ;
        for(ip=0;ip<np;ip++)
        tempp=aa[ip];
        printf("\n aa[%i] number =%i ", ip, tempp);
}
```

Output:

Array values are
aa[0] number=11
aa[1] number =12
aa[2] number =13
aa[3] number =14

8.10 Dynamic Memory Allocation (DMA)

The concept of **dynamic memory allocation in c language** *enables the C programmer to allocate memory at runtime.*

Or

The process of allocating memory at runtime or execution time is known as **dynamic memory allocation.** Library routines known as memory management functions are used for allocating and freeing memory during execution of a program. These functions are defined in **stdlib. h** or alloc. h

Dynamic memory allocation in C language is possible by 4 functions of stdlib. h header file.

1. malloc()
2. calloc()
3. realloc()
4. free()

Difference between static memory allocation and dynamic memory allocation.

static memory allocation	dynamic memory allocation
memory is allocated at compile time.	memory is allocated at run time.
memory can't be increased while executing program.	memory can be increased while executing program.
used in array.	used in linked list.

functions used for dynamic memory allocation.

malloc()	allocates single block of requested memory.
calloc()	allocates multiple blocks of requested memory.
realloc()	reallocates the memory occupied by malloc() or calloc() functions.
free()	frees the dynamically allocated memory.

Note: Dynamic memory allocation related function can be applied for any data type that's why dynamic memory allocation related functions return void*.

Memory Allocation Process

Global variables, **static** variables and program instructions get their memory in **permanent** storage area whereas **local** variables are stored in area called **Stack**. The memory space between these two region is known as **Heap** area. This region is used for dynamic memory allocation during execution of the program. The size of heap keep changing.

malloc()

malloc stands for "memory allocation".

The malloc() function allocates single block of requested memory at runtime. This function reserves a block of memory of given size and returns a pointer of type void. This means that we can assign it to any type of pointer using typecasting. It doesn't initialize memory at execution time, so it has garbage value initially. If it fails to locate enough space (memory) it returns a NULL pointer.

syntax

pointer=(casttype*)malloc(size in bytes)

Example

```
char *p;
p = (int*)malloc(100 * sizeof(char));//memory space allocated to variable p
free(p);//releases the memory allocated to variable x
```

This statement will allocate 100 bytes according to size of char respectively and the pointer points to the address of first byte of memory.

Example

```
#include <stdio. h>
#include <stdlib. h>
void main()
{
        int n, ii, *p, s = 0;
        printf("Enter how many values you want ");
        scanf("%i", &n);
        p= (int*) malloc(n * sizeof(int));//memory reserved using malloc( )
        if(p == NULL)
        {
                printf("Alas! Requested memory not reserved");
                exit(0);
        }
        printf("Enter %i array values ", n);
```

```
        for(ii= 0; ii<n; ii++)
        {
                scanf("%i", &p[ii]);
                s = s+p[ii];
        }
        printf("addition of all array values = %i", s);
        free(p);
}
```

calloc( ):

calloc stands for "contiguous allocation".

Calloc() is another memory allocation function that is used for allocating memory at runtime. **calloc** function is normally used for allocating memory to derived data types such as **arrays** and **structures**. The calloc() function allocates multiple block of requested memory.

It initially initialize (sets) all bytes to zero. If it fails to locate enough space(memory) it returns a NULL pointer. The only difference between malloc() and calloc() is that, malloc() allocates single block of memory whereas calloc() allocates multiple blocks of memory each of same size.

Syntax :

pointer = (casttype*)calloc(number of blocks/elements, size of a block/element);
calloc() required 2 arguments

Example:

```
int *a;
a=(int*)calloc(100, sizeof(int));       // 200 bytes if int size is 2 bytes
char *s;
s=(char*)calloc(500, sizeof(char));  // 500 bytes
```

Example

```
struct student
{
	char rollno[20], names[30];
	int age;
};
typedef struct student st;
st *s;
s = (st*)calloc(30, sizeof(st));
```

Example

```
#include <stdio. h>
#include <stdlib. h>
void main()
{
	int n, ii, *p, s = 0;
	printf("Enter how many values you want ");
	scanf("%i", &n);
	p= (int*)calloc(n, sizeof(int));//memory reserved using
	calloc()
	if(p == NULL)
	{
		printf("Alas! Requested memory not reserved");
		exit(0);
	}
	printf("Enter %i array values ", n);
	for(ii=0; ii<n; ii++)
	{
		scanf("%i", &p[ii]);
		s = s+p[ii];
	}
	printf("\naddition of all array values = %i", s);
	free(p);
	}
```

Output:

Enter how many values you want 3
Enter 3 array values 1 2 3
naddition of all array values =6

Diffrence between malloc() and calloc()

calloc()	malloc()
calloc() initializes the allocated memory with 0 value.	malloc() initializes the allocated memory with garbage values.
Number of arguments is 2	Number of argument is 1
Syntax: Pointer=(cast_type*) calloc(blocks, size_of_block);	**Syntax:** Pointer=(cast_type *)malloc(Size_ in_bytes);

realloc(): changes memory size that is already allocated to a variable.

Or

If the previously allocated memory is insufficient or more than required, you can change the previously allocated memory size using realloc().

- If memory is not sufficient for malloc() or calloc(), you can reallocate the memory by realloc() function. In short, it changes the memory size. By using realloc() we can create the memory dynamically at middle stage. Generally by using realloc() we can reallocation the memory. Realloc() required 2 arguments of type void*, size_type. Void* will indicates previous block base address, size-type is data type size. Realloc() will creates the memory in bytes format and initial value is garbage.

syntax

p=realloc(p, newsize in bytes);

Example:

```
int *xx;
xx=(int*)malloc(5 * sizeof(int));
xx=(int*)realloc(xx, 100);//allocated a new memory to variable xx
```

Example

```
void* realloc(void*, size-type);
int *a;
a=(int*)calloc(2, sizeof(int));
:
:
a=(int*)realloc(a, sizeof(int)*100);//reallocating the memory for a
```

Example Program:

```
#include <stdio. h>
#include <stdlib. h>
void main()
{
        int *p, j, m, n;
        printf("Enter array size: ");
        scanf("%i", &m);
        p= (int*) malloc(m* sizeof(int));
        printf("Addresses of reserved memory are: ");
        for(j= 0; j< m; j++)
        printf("%p\t", p+ j);
        printf("Enter array's new size: ");
        scanf("%i", &n);
        p = realloc(p, n);
        for(j= 0; j< n; j++)
        printf("%p\t", p+ j);
}
```

free()

When your program comes out, operating system automatically release all the memory allocated by your program but as a good practice when you are not in need of memory anymore then you should release that memory by calling the function free().

The memory occupied by malloc() or calloc() functions must be released by calling free() function. Otherwise, it will consume memory until program exit.

Or

Dynamically allocated memory created with either calloc() or malloc() doesn't get freed on its own. You must explicitly use free() to release the space.

Syntax:

free(pointer);

Example

```
#include <stdio. h>
#include <alloc. h>
void main()
{
        int n, ii, *p, s = 0;
        printf("Enter how many values you want ");
        scanf("%i", &n);
        p= (int*)calloc(n, sizeof(int));//memory reserved using
        calloc()
        if(p == NULL)
        {
                printf("Alas! Requested memory not reserved");
                exit(0);
        }
        printf("Enter %i array values ", n);
```

```
        for(ii=0; ii<n; ii++)
        {
                scanf("%i", &p[ii]);
                s = s+p[ii];
        }
        printf("\naddition of all array values = %i", s);
        free(p);
}
```

Output:

Enter how many values you want 3
Enter 3 array values 1 2 3
naddition of all array values =6

8.11 Command-Line Arguments

It is possible to pass some values from the command line to your C programs when they are executed. These values are called **command line arguments** and many times they are important for your program especially when you want to control your program from outside instead of hard coding those values inside the code.

The arguments passed from command line are called command line arguments. These arguments are handled by main() function.

To support command line argument, you need to change the structure of main() function

Syntax:

int main(**int** argc, **char** *argv[])

Here, **argc** counts the number of arguments. It counts the file name as the first argument.

The **argv[]** contains the total number of arguments. The first argument is the file name always.

Example1

```
#include <stdio. h>
int main(int a, char *ar[ ])
{
        int i;
        printf("\nThe no of arguments supplied is %i", a);
        printf("The command line arguments are:");
        for(i=0;i<a;i++)
        printf("\n %s", ar[i]);
}
```

Output:

```
C:\TC\BIN\myp. exe 10 a $
The no of arguments supplied is 4
The command line arguments are:
C:\TC\BIN\myp. exe
10
a
$
```

Example2

```
#include <stdio. h>
void main(int ac, char *av[ ])
{
        printf("\n executable Program name is: %s", av[0]);
        printf("\nFirst command line argument is: %s", av[1]);
}
}
```

Output

p. exe hit

```
executable Program name is: p. exe
First command line argument is: hit
```

Note

But if you pass many arguments within double quote, all arguments will be treated as a single argument only.

Example

```
C:\TC\BIN\myp. exe "10 a $"
executable Program name is: C:\TC\BIN\myp. exe
First command line argument is: 10 a $
```

Example 3

Write a C program to find all arithmetical operations using command line arguments

```
#include<stdio. h>
#include<stdlib. h>
void main(int ac, char* av[])
{
        int a, b;
        a=atoi(av[1]);
        b=atoi(av[2]);
        printf("\n addition value =%i", a+b);
        printf("\n subtraction value =%i", a-b);
        printf("\n multiplicaon value =%i", a*b);
        printf("\n division value =%i", a/b);
        printf("\n modulus division value =%i", a%b);
}
```

Output

```
C:/TC/BIN>TCC myp. c 10 20
addition value =30
subtraction value =-10
multiplicaon value =200
division value =0
modulus division value =1
```

Example4:

Write a C program to demonstrate the concept of command line arguments

```
#include<stdio. h>
void main(int x, char *y[ ])
{
        printf("\n Total number of arguments at the command prompt
        is %i", x);
        printf("\n file name is: %s ", y[0]);
        printf("\nfirst argument is %s ", y[1]);
        printf("\n second argument is %s", y[2]);
        printf("\nthird argument is %s ", y[3]);
        printf("fourth argument is %s ", y[4]);
        printf("\n fifth argument is %s ", y[5]);
}
```

Output

./a. out welcome to happy learning
Total number of arguments at the command prompt is 5
file name is./a. out
first argument is welcome
second argument is to
third argument is happy
fourth argument is learning
fifth argument is NULL

Explanation: In the above example.

x = 5
y[0] = "./a. out"
argv[1] = "welcome"
argv[2] = "to"
argv[3] = "happy"
argv[4] = "learning"
argv[5] = NULL

CHAPTER 9

Structures and Unions

9.1 Introduction

A variable is used to store different values of same data type but only one value it can hold at a time. An array is a derived data type which is derived from basic datatypes. Array is basically set or group of elements of same datatype under one name. The elements or values of an array accessed via index or position. But in real life, most of the data is heterogeneous only.

Examples:

Employee details like employee id, employee name, salary, age, mobile no, email, addres...

Book details like book title, book name, price, pages,...

Product details like product id, product name, product description,....

To handle heterogeneous data, C language has a concept called STRUCTURES.

Structure is a user defined datatype. It's nothing but collection of heterogeneous elements under a single name is called a structure. It is nothing but a record of a file or database.

Defining a Structure:

structure data type has to be defined before it is used in the program similar to variables, functions.
The general format for defining the structured data type is given below.

```
struct structurename
{
        data type variable 1;
        data type variable 2;
        :
        :
        data type variable n;
};
```

The *struct* is a keyword.

Structurename is a valid name like other programming elements names. It is also called tag or tag name of the structure. Data types such as int, float, char, double are allowed. variable 1, variable 2, variable 3,.... are any valid names. These are also called as members or fields. Every structure definition ends with ;

example:

```
struct student
{
        char roll_number[15];
        char name[30];
        int age;
        char address[100];
};
```

9.2 Declaring Structure Variables

Members of the structure cannot be accessed directly. To access the member of a structure within a program, a variable has to be declared. We can declare structure variables in two ways

Type 1:

```
struct structurename
{
        data type variable 1;
        data type variable 2;
        :
        :
        data type variable n
}var1, var2,.., varn;
```

Example:

```
struct student
{
        char roll_number[15];
        char name[30];
        int age;
        char address[100];
}a, b, c, d;
// a, b, c, d are variables of type struct student
```

Type 2:

```
struct student a, b, c, d;
// Here struct student is a user defined datatype and a, b, c, d are variables
```

9.3 Accessing Structure Members

The individual members of a structure can be accessed through the structure variables only. The link between a member and a variable is established through the operator '.' is called as the dot operator or member access operator or period operator.

The syntax is

Structure variable. Field name

Example:

```
struct student
{
        char roll_number[15];
        char name[30];
        int age;
        char address[100];
}a, b, c, d;
```

a. roll_number, b. name, c. age, d. address
similarly b. roll_number...

Note: it is possible to access all the members, through a single variable. There is no one to one correspondence between the the number of members to the number of variables. Any variable can access any member of the struct.

9.3.1 Assigning Values to the Members

Strings can't be assigned directly using = operator.
Members of the structure can be assigned the values as given below.

```
strcpy(a. roll_number, 2188aa0501);
strcpy(a. name, “sai”);
a. age = 17;
strcpy(a. address,”h. no: 1-1-1, dms illa, ts”);
```

scanf ( ), gets( ) can also be used to give values through the keyboard.

```
scanf(“%s”, a. roll_number);
scanf(“%s”, a. roll_name);
scanf(“%d”, & a. age);
scanf(“%s”, a. address);
```

9.3.2 Structure Initialization

Like any other data type, a structure variable can be initialized at compile time. The general format for structure initialization is struct structure_name variablename = { v1, v2,......, vn};

where v1, v2,...., vn are the values of the fields, field1, field2,...fieldn respectively. The values are separated by commas.

Consider the following example 1:

```
struct data
{
        char x;
        int y;
        float z;
}a, b;
struct values a = {'q', 1, 1. 8};
struct values b= {'w', 90, 2. 1};
```

example 2:

```
struct data
{
        char x;
        int y;
        float z;
}a={'q', 1, 1. 8}, b= {'w', 90, 2. 1};
```

Basic programs:

1. Write a C program to create a record called item with id, name, cost, qty as fields and then read, display one record details.

```
#include<stdio. h>
struct product
{
        int id;
        char pname[40];
        float cost;
        int qty;
}a;
```

```
void main( )
{
        printf("\n pls enter product's id, name, cost and quantity: ");
        scanf("%i %s %f %i", &a. id, a. pname, &a. cost,&a. qty);
        printf("\n product details are");
        printf("\n product's id= %i", a. id);
        printf("\n product's name: %s", a. pname);
        printf("\n product's cost is: %f", a. cost);
        printf("\n product's quantity is: %i", a. qty);
}
```

Result:

Input:
pls enter product's id, name, cost and quantity: 11
paste
123. 98
120

Output:
product details are
product's id= 11
product's name: paste
product's cost is: 123. 98
product's quantity is: 120

2. Write a C program to demonstrate the usage of accessing structure members

```
#include <stdio. h>
struct anand
{
        int a; int b; int c;
};
void main ( )
{
        struct anand p;
```

```
        p. a = 99;
        p. b = 20;
        p. c = 3.
        printf("\n a =%i\t b=%i\t c=%i", p. a, p. b, p. c);
}
```

Output:

a =99   b=20   c=3

3. Write a program to process one student record with members rollnumber, student name, age, address and mobile number.

```
#include <stdio. h>
struct student
{
        char roll_number[15];
        char nam[30];
        int ag;
        char addresss[100];
        long int mno;
}ab;
void main()
{
        printf("\n enter the roll number name of the student: ");
        gets(ab. roll_number);
        printf("\n enter the name of the student: ");
        gets(ab. nam);
        printf("\n enter the age of the student: ");
        scanf("%i", &ab. age);
        printf("\n enter the adderess of the student: ");
        scanf("%s", ab. addresss);
        printf("\n enter the mobile number of the student: ");
        scanf("%ld", &ab. mno);
        printf("\n Roll number of the student: %s", ab. roll_number);
        printf("\n name of the student: %s ", ab. nam);
        printf("\n age of the student: %i", ab. age);
```

```
        printf("\n adderess of the student: %s ", ab. address);
        printf("\nmobile number of the student: %ld", ab. mno);
}
```

Output:

enter the roll number name of the student:
123
enter the name of the student:
anand vihan
enter the age of the student: 17
enter the adderess of the student: 1-1-1, doms adda, ts
enter the mobile number of the student: 12367890
roll number name of the student: 123
name of the student: anand vihan
age of the student: 17
adderess of the student: 1-1-1, doms adda, ts
mobile number of the student: 12367890

9.4 Arrays of Structures

Array of structures to store much information of different data types. Each element of the array representing a **structure** variable. The array of structures is also known as collection of structures.

Ex: if you want to handle more records within one structure, we need not specify the number of structure variable. Simply we can use array of structure variable to store them in one structure variable.

Example: struct employee emp[5];

Example of structure with array that stores information of 5 students and prints it.

```
#include<stdio. h>
#include<conio. h>
#include<string. h>
struct student{
```

```
int rollno;
char name[10];
};
void main(){
int i;
struct student st[5];
clrscr();
printf("Enter Records of 5 students");
for(i=0;i<5;i++){
printf("\nEnter Rollno:");
scanf("%d",&st[i]. rollno);
printf("\nEnter Name:");
scanf("%s",&st[i]. name);
}
printf("\nStudent Information List:");
for(i=0;i<5;i++){
printf("\nRollno:%d, Name:%s", st[i]. rollno, st[i]. name);
}
getch();
}
```

Output:

```
Enter Records of 5 students
Enter Rollno: 1
Enter Name: Vijay
Enter Rollno: 2
Enter Name: Rajni
Enter Rollno: 3
Enter Name: Ajith
Enter Rollno: 4
Enter Name: Stalin
Enter Rollno: 5
Enter Name: Dhanush
Student Information List:
```

Rollno: 1, Name: Vijay
Rollno: 2, Name: Rajni
Rollno: 3, Name: Ajith
Rollno: 4, Name: Stalin
Rollno: 5, Name: Dhanush

Exercise:

1. Write a C program to create a structure called student with fields rollno, name, age, gender and marks in three subjects. Your program should process n number of student details and it should find average marks of the students.
2. Write a C program to create a structure called employee with members employee_id, name, salary. Your program should process n number of student details and it should find average marks of the employees.
3. Write a C program to define a structure called item with members item_id, name and price. Your program should process n number of item details and it should find costliest item and cheapest item.

9.5 Nested Structures

structure can have another structure as a member. There are two ways to define nested structure in c language:

1. By separate structure
2. By Embedded structure

1) Separate structure

We can create 2 structures, but dependent structure should be used inside the main structure as a member. Let's see the code of nested structure.

struct Date
{

```
        int dd;
        int mm;
        int yyyy;
};

struct Employee
{
        int id;
        char name[20];
        struct Date doj;
}emp1;
```

2) Embedded structure

```
struct Employee
{
        int id;
        char name[20];
        struct Date
        {
                int dd;
                int mm;
                int yyyy;
        }doj;
}emp1;
```

Accessing Nested Structure

We can access the member of nested structure by Outer_Structure. Nested_Structure. member as given below:

```
e1. doj. dd
e1. doj. mm
e1. doj. yyyy
```

Example program: on Nested Structures

```
#include<stdio. h>
struct Employee
{
        int id;
        char name[20];
        struct Date
        {
                int dd;
                int mm;
                int yyyy;
        }doj;
}emp1;
void main()
{
        printf("\n enter employee id");
        scanf("%d",&emp1. id);
        printf("\n enter employee name");
        gets(emp1. name);
        printf("\n enter employee date of joining");
        scanf("%d%d%d",&emp1. doj. dd,& emp1. doj. mm ,&emp1.
        doj. yyyy);
        printf("\nemployeid=%d, name=%s, date of joining=%d-%d-
        %d", emp1. id, emp1. name,, emp1. doj. dd, emp1. doj. mm ,
        emp1. doj. yyyy);
}
```

Difference Between Array and Structure

1	Array is collection of homogeneous data.	Structure is the collection of heterogeneous data.
2	Array data are access using index.	Structure elements are access using . operator.

3	Array allocates static memory.	Structures can allocate dynamic memory.
4	Array element access takes less time than structures.	Structure elements take more time than Array.

9.6 Structures and Functions

We can pass structure as an argument to a function in two ways

1. Passing individual members of the structure as an argument.
2. Passing the entire structure as an argument.

Passing individual members of the structure as an argument:

For example the structure is

```
struct pen
{
        char name[20];
        float price;
        int quantity;
};
```

And it is initialized in the following way

```
struct pen p={“parker”, 125. 46, 100};
```

We can pass this structure to the function display() by passing the individual members as arguments in the following way

```
display(p. name, p. price, p. quantity);
```

Program:

```
#include<stdio. h>
struct pen
{
        char name[20];
        float price;
        int quantity;
};
```

```
struct pen p={"parker", 125. 46, 100};
void display(char x[], float y, int z);
void main()
{
        display(p. name, p. price, p. quantity);
}
void display(char x[], float y, int z)
{
        printf("\n pen name=%s\n pen price=%f \n quantity=%d", x, y, z);
}
```

Passing the entire structure as an argument:

Passing the structure variable is nothing but passing the whole or entire structure.

Program:

```
#include<stdio. h>
struct pen
{
        char name[20];
        float price;
        int quantity;
};
struct pen p={"parker", 125. 46, 100};// p is structure variable
void display(struct pen x);// passing a structure variable
void main()
{
        display(p);
}
void display(struct pen x)
{
        printf("\npenname=%s\n pen price=%f \n quantity=%d", x.
        name, x. price, x. quantity);
}
```

9.7 Structures and Pointers

We can declare a pointer variable to point the structure.

Example:

```
struct pen
{
        char name[20];
        float price;
        int quantity;
};
struct pen a,*p;// here p is of type struct pen
p=&s;
```

To access the members of a structure through pointer variable, we use -> (array) operator.

Program:

```
#include<stdio. h>
struct pen
{
        char name[20];
        float price;
        int quantity;
};
struct pen a={"parker", 125. 46, 100},*p=&a;// p is structure variable
void main()
{
        printf("\npenname=%s\n pen price=%f \n quantity=%d", p.
        name, p. price, p. quantity);
}
```

9.8 Self Referential Structures

It is a structure which contains a pointer variable as a member to it. This pointer variable used store the address of another variable of same structure type. Self referential structures are also called liked lists.

Example:

```
struct student
{
        int age;
        struct student *p;// p is pointer of type struct student
}s1, s2;
```

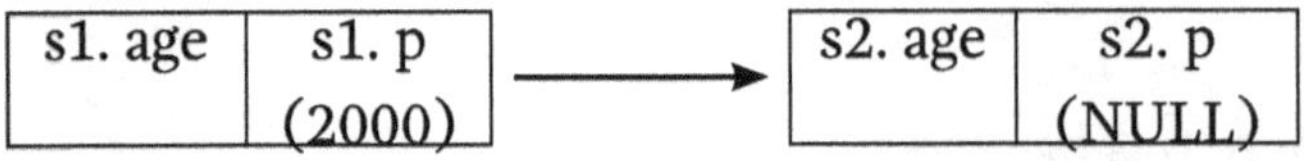

s1. age	s1. p (2000)	⟶	s2. age	s2. p (NULL)

address → 1000 2000

In lined list or self referential structures every element is called a node. Every node contains a data field and pointer field. In the above example data field is age and pointer filed is p used store address of immediate next node. In the linked list, last node pointer contains only NULL to indicates no nodes are thereafter.

Program:

```
#include<stdio. h>
struct student
{
        int age;
        struct student *p;// p is pointer of type struct student
}*t, head=*tail=NULL;
void main()
{
        int n;
        printf(" how many details you want to enter");
        scanf("%d",&n);
        while(n>0)
{
        t=(struct student *)malloc(sizeof(struct student));
```

```
        printf("\n enter student age");
        scanf("%d",&t->age);
        t->p=NULL;
        if(head==NULL)
        head=tail=t;
        else
        {
                tail->p=t;
                tail=t;
        }
        n--;
}
        printf("The student details are");
        t=head;
        while(t!=NULL)
        {
                printf("\n age=%d", t->age);
                t=t->p;
        }
}
```

9.9 Unions

Union is also like a structure used to create user defined datatypes. It is collection of heterogeneous elements under a single name.

Characteristics of Union:

- The size of a union equal to maximum member's size.
- Ex: union num

```
{
        char name[10];
        int age;
        Float price;
};
```

- In this example union size is 10 bytes because name member occupies more memory than other members.
- All the members of a union share a common storage area or memory.
- All the members of a union can't be accessed at a time.

Union Declaration:

Similar to structure, union can be declared

Syntax: union union_name

```
{
        Datatype member1;
        Datatype member2;
        :
        :
        Datatype member;
};
```

Ex: union num

```
{ int x;char y;float z;
};
```

Union variable Declaration:

Syntax: union union_name variable;
Ex: union num a, b, c;

Accessing the members of a Union:

Syntax: variable. member;
Ex: a. x;

Program:

Write a C program to demo the use of unions

```
#include<stdioh>
void main()
```

```
{
        union num
        {
                char ch;
                int n;
        }p;// unions and structures can be declared inside main() also
        p. ch='A';
        printf("\n p. ch value=%c", p. ch);// output: A
        p. ch=300;
        printf("\n p. n value=%d", p. n);//output: 300
        printf("\n p. ch value=%d", p. ch);// output: 44
        p. ch='A';
        printf("\n p. ch value=%d", p. ch);// output: A
        printf("\n p. n value=%d", p. n);//output: 321
}
```

9.10 Bit Fields

Bit fields are used to reserve the memory in terms of bits. This concept is used when memory is limited and want to store Boolean values like true(1), false(0).

- Bit fields must be a member of structure or union.
- The address of bit fields can't be accessed.
- Bit fields denote the length of a member in terms of bits only.
- Syntax:
  data type member: bit field length;
- Ex: struct date
  ```
  {
          int day, month, year;
  };
  ```
  This structure occupies 6 bytes of memory.
- The same structure can be declared with bit fields concept
  ```
  struct date
  {
  ```

```
        unsigned int day: 5;// 5 bits
        unsigned int month: 4;
        unsigned int year: 7;
    };
```

- Now This structure occupies only 16 bits(2 bytes).

Program:

Write a C program to demo the use of bit fields.

```
#include<stdio. h>
void main()
{
    struct date
{
    unsigned int day: 5;// 5 bits
    unsigned int month: 4;
    unsigned int year: 7;
}d={3, 2, 82};
printf("date:%d-%d-%d", d. day, d. month, d. year);
}
```

9.11 Typedef

This is used to create alias names for the existing datatypes.

Syntax:

typedef existing_data_type new_datatype;
Ex1: typedef int CM_Jagan;
Ex2: typedef struct student YSRCP;

9.12 Enumerations (enum)

It is a keyword used to create user defined data type and used to represent limited values.

Syntax: enum tagname{ set of enumerators};

- enum is a keyword
- tagname is an identifier
- enumerator is variable use to used to store an integer value.
- The default initial value of a first enumerator is 0(zero)and the remaining enumerators value incremented by one(1) in a sequence.
- Ex: enum months{jan, feb, mar};// jan value =0, feb value=1, mar value=2

  enum values{a=5, b, c, i=-4, j};//it is a valid statement. a=5, b=6, c=7, i=-4, j=-3

Program:

Write a C program to demonstrate the use of enum keyword

```
#include<stdio. h>
void main()
{
        enum values{a=5, b, c, i=-4, j};
        printf("\n a value=%d", a);
        printf("\n b value=%d", b);
        printf("\n c value=%d", c);
        printf("\n i value=%d", i);
        printf("\n j value=%d", j);
}
```

CHAPTER 10

Files

10.1 Introduction

So far we have used printf(), scanf() functions for writing and reading the data. These functions are called console oriented i/o functions which deal with console (ex: keyboard, monitor). However in real life problems, we need to handle large amount of data. But these console oriented functions can't deal large amount of data and faces two problems mainly.

- Difficult to handle and time consuming process to read and write huge amount of data.
- The data is lost whenever the program is terminated or power turned off.

To overcome these two problems C has a concept in the name of FILES to store large amount of data.

FILES:

File is a set of records which contain set of related fields. File is a place on a secondary storage device where a group of related data is stored.

Ex: student's file

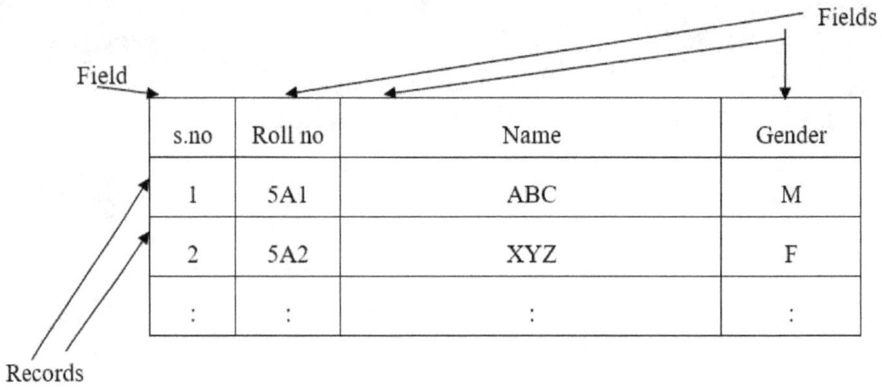

Field → ; Fields → ; Records →

s.no	Roll no	Name	Gender
1	5A1	ABC	M
2	5A2	XYZ	F
:	:	:	:

Types of Files: Based on content or data of a file. Files are two types

- Text files
- Binary files

Text files:

Text files contain data in the form of letters, digits or special symbols which can be read and understand by humans.

Ex: abc. txt, c7p1. c, p. dat

Binary files:

Binary files contain data in the form of bits that can be easily understood by computers and not by humans.

Ex: 1. exe. xyz. dll// exe means executable files

Based accessing the file data, files are two types

- Sequential access files
- Random access files

Sequential access files:

If the records of a file accessed one after another in a sequence, Then such file is called sequential access file.

Random access files:

If the records of a file accessed directly or randomly, Then such file is called Random access file.

To use files, there three actions should be carried out.

- Defining and opening a file
- Process the file
- Close the file

10.2 Defining and Opening a File

If we want to store data on a file, we must specify certain things about a file to an operating system. Those are

- File name
- Structure
- Purpose

Filename:

It is a valid identifier for the operating system. Generally the file name contains two parts

- Primary name
- Optional period with an extension.

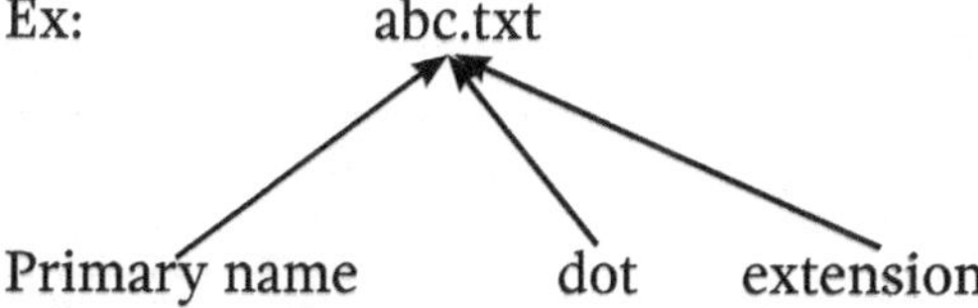

Structure:

The structure of a file is defined in stdio. h header file as FILE. All the files must be declared of FILE type. When we want to open a file, we should specify what we want to do with that file.

For example, we can open a file for writing data or reading the data.

Syntax:

FILE *filepointer_variable;
Filepointer_variable=fopen("filename","mode");

Ex: FILE *p;
p=fopen("x. c","r");

1. fopen(): it is a function that sends a request to the operating system to open a particular file, then the operating system searches the requested file on the disk. If the file exists, then file pointer (ex: p)points the first character of a requested file(file pointer contains address of first byte of the file).
   Ex: x. c

p

```
// this is a C program
#include<stdio. h>
void main()
{
    :
    :
}
```

And the file pointer value automatically incremented while doing the operations like reading, writing, Etc.

Text files modes:

S. no	Mode	Symbol	Purpose	Example
1	Write	"w"	It opens a file for writing purpose. If already the file exists then the file contents will be overwritten otherwise a new file will be created.	P=fopen("x. txt","w");

2	Read	"r"	It opens a file for reading purpose. If already the file exists then the file contents will be read one by one by the file pointer otherwise fopen() returns NULL.	P=fopen("x. txt","r");
3	Append	"a"	It opens a file for appending purpose. If already the file exists then the file contents will be added at the end of the file otherwise a newfile will be created.	P=fopen("x. txt","a");
Text files mixed modes:				
1	Write+read	"w+"	It opens a file for writing and reading purpose. If already the file exists then the file contents will be overwritten otherwise a new file will be created.	P=fopen("x. txt","w+");
2	Append+read	"a+"	It opens a file for appending and reading purpose. If already the file exists then the file contents will be added at the end of the file otherwise a new file will be created.	P=fopen("x. txt","a+");

Continued...

3	Read+write	"r+"	It opens a file for reading and writing purpose. If already the file exists then the file contents will be read one by one by the file pointer otherwise fopen() returns NULL.	P=fopen("x. txt","r+");

Binary files modes:

S. no	Mode	Symbol	Purpose	Example
1	Write	"wb"	It opens a file for writing purpose. If already the file exists then the file contents will be overwritten otherwise a new file will be created.	P=fopen("x. txt","wb");
2	Read	"rb"	It opens a file for reading purpose. If already the file exists then the file contents will be read one by one by the file pointer otherwise fopen() returns NULL.	P=fopen("x. txt","rb");
3	Append	"ab"	It opens a file for appending purpose. If already the file exists then the file contents will be added at the end of the file otherwise a newfile will be created.	P=fopen("x. txt","ab");

Binary files mixed modes:				
1	Write+read	"w+b"	It opens a file for writing and reading purpose. If already the file exists then the file contents will be overwritten otherwise a new file will be created.	P=fopen("x. txt","w+b");
2	Append+read	"a+b"	It opens a file for appending and reading purpose. If already the file exists then the file contents will be added at the end of the file otherwise a new file will be created.	P=fopen("x. txt","a+b");
3	Read+write	"r+b"	It opens a file for reading and writing purpose. If already the file exists then the file contents will be read one by one by the file pointer otherwise fopen() returns NULL.	P=fopen("x. txt","r+b");

10.3 Closing a File

The opened file can be closed by fclose() function.

Syntax: fclose(file pointer);

Ex: fclose(p);// closes only one file
fcloseall();//closes all opened files

10.4 File Input and Output Functions

To process the files for various operations, we use file input and output functions. These are two types

- Formatted file input and output functions.
- Unformatted file input and output functions.

Formatted file input and output functions:

These functions deal with format specifiers in which format the data has to be written and accepted. The functions are

- fprintf () function: This function works similar to printf() to write the data on a screen or a file.
  Syntax: fprintf (fileponiter,”format specifiers”, variables);
  Ex: fprintf (fp,”%d%c”, a, b);// writes a, b values into a file
  fprintf (stdout,”%d%c”, a, b);//displays a, b values on screen
  // stdout is a standard output stream
- fscanf () function: This function works similar to scanf() to read the data from a file or a keyboard.
  Syntax: fscanf(fileponiter,”format specifiers”,&variables);
  Ex: fscanf(fp,”%d%c”,&a,&b);// reads a, b values from a file
  fscanf(stdin,”%d%c”,&a,&b);//reads a, b values from a keyboard
  // stdin is a standard input stream. stream is temporary buffer.

Program:

Write a C program to read the data from the keyboard write that in a file and again read the data from a file, write that on a screen.

```
#include<stdio. h>
void main( )
{
        char ch;
        int a;
        float b;
        FILE *fp;
        fp=fopen(“x. txt”.”w”);
        printf(“enter ch, a, b values”);
        fscanf(stdin,”%c%d%f”,&ch,&a,&b);
```

```
        fprintf(fp,"%c%d%f", ch, a, b);
        fclose(fp);
        fp=fopen("x. txt"."r");
        printf("\n The file contents:");
        fscanf(fp,"%c%d%f",&ch,&a,&b);
        fprintf(stdout,"%c%d%f", ch, a, b);
        fclose(fp);
}
```

Unformatted file input and output functions:

s. no	Function	Purpose	Syntax	Example
1	fgetc()	Used to read a single character from a file	fgetc(filepointer);	fgetc(fp);
2	fputc()	Used to write a single character on a file	fputc(variable, filepointer);	fputc(v, fp);

Program:

Write a C program to copy the contents of one file into another file.

```
#include<stdio. h>
void main( )
{
        char ch;
        FILE *fp1,*fp2;
        fp1=fopen("x. txt","r");
        fp2=fopen("y. txt","w");
        if(fp1==NULL)
        printf("\n file does not exist");
        else
        {
                while((ch=fgetc(fp1))!=EOF)
                { fputc(ch, fp2);
        }
```

```
        fcloseall();
    }
}
```

Exercise:

1. Write a C program to check whether the two files are identical or not.
2. Write a C program to count number of occurrences of a particular character in a file.
3. Write a C program to count number of occurrences of a particular word in a file.
4. Write a C program to count number of characters, words, lines in a file.
5. Write a C program to count number of vowels in a file.
6. Write a C program to merge the contents of two files.

s. no	Function	Purpose	Syntax	Example
3	fgets()	Used to read a string of specified size from a file. It stops reading when it encounters a newline character.	fgets(variable, size, filepointer);	fgets(v, 50, fp);
4	fputs()	Used to write a string on a file	fputs(variable, filepointer);	fputs (v, fp);

Program:

Write a C program to demonstrate the use of fgets(), fputs() functions

```
#include<stdio. h>
void main( )
{
    char msg[100];
    FILE *fp;
    fp=fopen("x. txt","r");
    if(fp==NULL)
```

```
        printf("\n file does not exist");
        else
        {
                fgets(msg, 20, fp);
                printf("\n The message is:");
                fputs(msg, stdout);
                fclose(fp);
        }
}
```

s. no	Function	Purpose	Syntax	Example
5	getw()	Used to read an integer from a file.	getw(filepointer);	getw(fp);
6	putw()	Used to write an integer on a file	putw(variable, filepointer);	putw (v, fp);

Program:

A file called x. dat contains series of integers. Write a C program to copy all the even numbers into a file called p. dat and odd numbers into a file called q. dat.

```
#include<stdio. h>
void main( )
{
        FILE *fp1,*fp2,*fp3;
        int n, i;
        fp1=fopen("x. txt","w");
        for(i=1;i<=100;i++)
        putw(i, fp1);
        fclose(fp1);
        fp1=fopen("x. txt","r");
        if(fp1==NULL)
        printf("\n file does not exist");
        else
        {
```

```
            fp2=fopen("p. dat","w");
            fp3=fopen("q. dat","w");
            while((n=getw(fp1))!=EOF)
            {
                    if(n%2==0)
                    putw(n, fp2);
                    else
                    putw(n, fp3);
            }
        fcloseall();
        }
}
```

Binary file input and output functions:

These functions are also called block i/o functions or direct i/o functions

s. no	Function	Purpose	Syntax	Example
1	fread()	Used to read a record from a file.	fread(&structure, size of the structure, number of records, filepointer);	fread(&s, sizeof(s), 2, fp);
2	fwrite()	Used to write a record on a file	fwrite(&structure, size of the structure, number of records, filepointer);	fwrite(&s, sizeof(s), 2, fp);

Program:

1. Write a C program to process n records into a file. A record contains the following fields rollno, age, name.

```
#include<stdio. h>
#include<string. h>
void main( )
```

```
{
        FILE *fp;
        Struct student
        {
                char rollno[10];
                int age;
                char name[20];
        }s;
        int n, i;
        fp=fopen("x. txt","wb");
        if(fp==NULL)
        printf("\n file does not exist");
        else
        {
                printf("\n how many student records you want to
                rocess");
                scanf("%d",&n);
                for(i=1;i<=n;i++)
                {
                        printf("\n enter student rollno, age, name");
                        fflush(stdin);
                        gets(s. rollno);
                        fflush(stdin);
                        scanf("%d",&s. age);
                        fflush(stdin);
                        gets(s. name);
                        fwrite(&s, sizeof(s), 1, fp);
                        fcloseall();
                }
                fp=fopen("x. txt","rb");
                if(fp==NULL)
                printf("\n file does not exist");
                else
```

```
        {
        printf("\n The student records are");
        for(i=1;i<=n;i++)
                {
                fread(&s, sizeof(s), 1, fp);
                printf("\n student rollno=%s\t age=%d\
                tname=%s", s. rollno, s. age, s. name);
                fcloseall();
                }
        }
}
```

Exercise:

1. Write a C program to process n employee records into a file. A record contains the following fields employee_id, name, salary and find average salary also.

10.5 Random Access Functions

So far we used various functions to read the data from a file or write the data into a file. But, in some situations we are interested to read a particular record from a file. To achieve this, we use random access functions.

The random access functions are

- ftell()
- rewind()
- fseek()

ftell(): This returns the current position of the file pointer in terms of long integer value.

Syntax: ftell(filepointer);

Example:

x. txt file

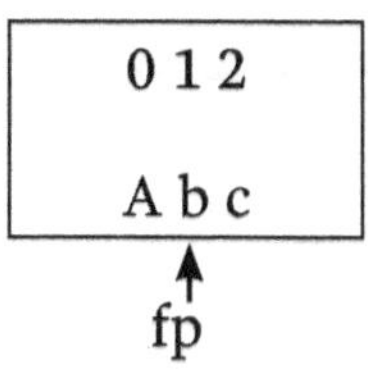

n=ftell(fp);

n value is 2// the first byte of the file is numbered as zero(0), the next one is one(1) and so on.

rewind():

This function moves the file pointer to the beginning of the file.

Synatx: rewind(filepointer);

Example:

x. txt file

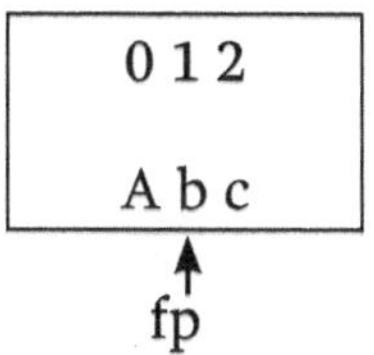

rewind(fp);

//after rewind operation, the filepointer(fp) is

x. txt file

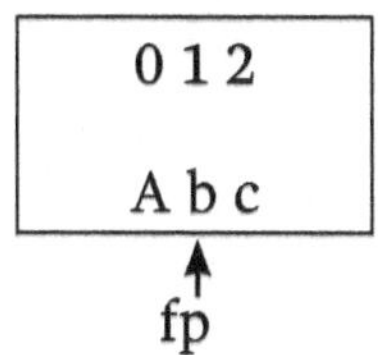

fseek():

This function moves the file pointer to a desired position or particular position in a file.

Syntax:

fseek(filepointer, offset, position);

- **file pointer:** it is a pointer to a file
- **offset:** it can be a long integer variable or number that specifies how many bytes to be moved from a position of a file. It can be positive or negative. If it is positive then it indicates forward move otherwise backward move.
- **Position:** It is an integer value that takes one of the three values

Value	meaning
0	Beginning of the file
1	present position of the file
2	end of the file

Examples:

Statement	**meaning**
fseek(fp, 0L, 0);	Beginning of the file
fseek(fp, 0L, 2);	end of the file
fseek(fp, m, 0);	moves the file pointer by m bytes from the beginning.
fseek(fp, m, 1);	moves the file pointer by m bytes from current position.
fseek(fp,-m, 1);	moves the file pointer by m bytes backward from current position.

Program:

1. Write a C program to demonstrate the use of ftell(), rewind(), fseek() functions.

```
#include<stdio. h>
#include<string. h>
void main( )
{
        FILE *fp;
        char ch;
        long int n;
        fp=fopen("x. txt","w+");
        printf("\n enter text, press ctrl+z to stop");
        while((ch=getchar())!=EOF)
        fputc(ch, fp);
        printf("\n the number of characters entered is %ld", ftell(fp));
        rewind(fp);
        printf("\n how many characters you want to skip");
        scanf("%ld"<&n);
        fseek(fp, n, 0);
        printf("\n file contents");
        while((ch=fgetc(fp))!=EOF)
        fputc(ch, stdout);
        fclose(fp);
}
```

2. Write a C program to display the contents of a file in reverse.

```
#include<stdio. h>
void main( )
{
        FILE *fp;
        char ch;
        fp=fopen("x. txt","r");
        fseek(fp, 0L, 2);
```

```
        fseek(fp,-1L, 1);
        while(ftell(fp)>=0)
        {
                ch=fgetc(fp);
                printf("%c", ch);
                fseek(fp,-2L, 1);
        }
        fclose(fp);
}
```

10.6 Error Handling Functions

There is a possibility of errors may occur during file processing. The possibilities are

When we try to

- Open a file with invalid name
- Opening a file which does not exist.
- Read the file beyond EOF character.
- Open a file for one operation but try to use for other operation.

To handle the errors in files, error handling functions are available in stdio. h header file. They are

feof():

This function used to detect the EOF character. If EOF character detected then it returns a non zero value otherwise zero.

Syntax:

feof(file pointer);
Example: feof(fp);

ferror():

This function used to detect the errors in the files. If error is occurred during file processing then it returns a non zero value otherwise zero.

Syntax:

ferror(file pointer);
Example: ferror(fp);

Program:

Write a C program to demonstrate the use of error handling functions.

```
#include<stdio. h>
void main( )
{
	FILE *fp;
	char ch[80];
	fp=fopen("x. txt","r");
	while(!feof(fp))
	{
		fscanf(fp,"%s", ch);
		if(ferror(fp)
		printf("\n error occurred");
		else
		printf("\n%s", ch);
	}
	fclose(fp);
}
```

Note: All file input/out functions (both formatted and unformatted), random access functions and error handling functions are file handling functions only.

Glossary

A

Actual arguments 163
Algorithm 29
Analog computers 19
Applications of an array 125
Arithmetic logic unit 12
Arithmetic operators 57
Array 119
Array of strings 153
Array of structures 216
Assignment operators 65

B

Binary file 232
Binary file modes 236
Bitfields 227
Bitwise operators 59

C

C character set 42
C ternary operator 66
C Tokens 44
Called function 160
Calling function 160
Categories of user defined functions 165
Central processing unit 11
Properties of a computer 1
Classification of computers 19
Client server computing environment 24
Command line arguments 204
Computer 1
Conditional Statements 87
Control unit 13
Creating and running a C program 55

D

Dangling else problem 92
Data types 49
Different statements 85
Digital computers 20
Distributed computing environment 25
Do while loop 105
Dynamic memory allocation 196

E

Enum 228
Expressions &its evaluation 68

F

File lnput output functions 237
Files 231
Flow chart 34
Flow chart symbols 34
For loop 106
Formal arguments 163
Function definition 162
Function prototype 160
Function 157
Function call 161
Function declaration 160

H

Hardcopy
Hardware 11
High level language 26
Hybrid computers 20

I

If else if ladder statement 92
If else statement 89
If statement 87
Increment & decrement operators 61
Input devices 14
Input ouput statements 72

J

Jump statements 116

L

Logical operators 59
Looping statements 99
Low level language 26

M

Mainframe computer 21
Major components 11
Memory unit 11
Middle level language 27
Mini computer 22
Multi dimensional arrays 141

N

Nested loops 112
Nested structures 218
Null pointer 188

O

One dimensional arrays 119
Operator precedence in C 67
Output devices 14

P

Parameter passing techniques 171
Personal computing environment 24
Pointer declaration 185
Pointer expression 190
Pointer and arrays 194
Pointer and functions 193
Pointer arithmetic 191
Primary storage devices 15
Program development life cycle 37

R
Random access file 233
Random access functions 244
Recursion 173
Relational operators 58
Return statement 161

S
Secondary storage devices 16
sequential access file 232
Softcopy 11
Software development lifecycle 37
Software 16
statement 85
storage classes 177
Storage devices 11
Storage unit 12
string handling functions 147
structure initialization 212
structures 209
structure of a C program 53
structures and functions 221
structures and pointers 223
Super computers 20
switch statement 96

T
Text file modes 234
Text file 232
Time sharing environment 25
Two dimensional arrays 131
Type conversion 83
Typedef 228
Types of statements 85

U
Unions 225

W
While loop 101

www.ingramcontent.com/pod-product-compliance
Lightning Source LLC
LaVergne TN
LVHW041203050326
832903LV00020B/440

* 9 7 8 1 6 3 9 0 4 5 2 9 7 *